IMAGES
of America

UKRAINIANS OF GREATER PHILADELPHIA

Bishop Soter Ortynsky, OSBM (1866–1916), the first bishop (1907–1916) of all Ukrainian and Ruthenian Greek Catholics in the United States, was born in Galicia, Ukraine, and he joined the Order of St. Basil the Great in 1884. He was elevated to the seat of bishop by Metropolitan Andrej Sheptytsky, OSBM, in 1907. While he was initially under the jurisdiction of the local Roman Catholic bishops in the United States of America, in 1913 he received from Rome the title of full exarch, responsible directly to Pope Pius X, with his seat in Philadelphia. His see became the hub of all Ukrainian religious and communal activities. Among his major accomplishments were inviting the Sisters of St. Basil the Great to the United States and founding an orphanage; establishing an evening school for cantors; organizing Prosvita (enlightenment society) reading rooms; and founding several newspapers, including *Rusin*, *America*, *Dushpastyr*, and *Eparchialny Vistnyk*. Recognizing the need for a fraternal society, he established the Providence Association of Ukrainian Catholics (Providence). All Ukrainian political, economic, social, and cultural activities were headed from his chancery on Franklin Street, making this thoroughfare the center of all Ukrainian life, not only in Philadelphia but also throughout the United States. To this day, it is the center of Ukrainian Catholic activity in Philadelphia.

On the cover: The Ukrainian American String Band performs a Kozak dance in the Mummers Parade on New Year's Day, 1964. Stanley Wolfe's original band started with a few West Philadelphia Ukrainian organizations, especially the American Ukrainian League of Fairmount, which was their headquarters in 1947. The Ukrainian American String Band performs not only for the New Year's Day extravaganza but participates in American as well as Ukrainian parades, concerts, and club events. (Author's collection.)

IMAGES
of America

UKRAINIANS OF GREATER PHILADELPHIA

Alexander Lushnycky, Ph.D.

ARCADIA
PUBLISHING

Published by Arcadia Publishing
Charleston, South Carolina

Printed in the United States of America

Library of Congress Catalog Card Number: 2007922520

For all general information contact Arcadia Publishing at:
Telephone 843-853-2070
Fax 843-853-0044
E-mail sales@arcadiapublishing.com
For customer service and orders:
Toll-Free 1-888-313-2665

Visit us on the Internet at www.arcadiapublishing.com

Dedicated to you in the future from us in the past

CONTENTS

ACKNOWLEDGMENTS

First and foremost, I want to thank the Providence Association of Ukrainian Catholics and its newspaper photograph files of the Ukrainian Catholic *America*. They were indispensable to the completion of this book. Secondly, I would like to thank Alexander Solowij of Meva Photo Video Studio, the longest and most professional Ukrainian photographer in Philadelphia, for chronicling the Ukrainian community and having perhaps the most valued repository of photographs on file, many of which I was unable to utilize for such a concise project. I also would like to thank Ukrainian Heritage Studies Center of Manor College, Manor Library, the Sisters of St. Basil the Great, Treasury of Faith Archieparchial Museum, Ukrainian Museum and Archives in Stamford, and holdings of Ukrainian Educational and Cultural Center, Ukrainian American Youth Association, the *Way*, Moloda Prosvita, St. Sophia's Religious Association of Ukrainian Catholics, Ukrainian Engineers' Society of America, and respective Ukrainian American clubs: Ukrainian American Citizens' Association and Ukrainian American League.

Others who assisted in the collection of rare photographs and materials were Vera Andryczyk, Dzinka Barabakh, Metodij Borecky, Ihor Chyzowych, Ivan Dubil, Marie Hanusey, Stefan Hawrysz, Orysia Hewka, Oksana Horajeckyj, Petro Hursky, Lew Iwaskiw, Maria and Mykola Kasian, Bohdan Kernytsky, Petro Kluk, Maria Kolybabiuk, Eryna Cvikula-Korchynska, Ivan Krych, Bohdan Kulchyckyj, Zenon Kwit, Larissa Kyj, Roman Lewyckyj, Lesia Leskiw, Pastor Dmytro Login, Michael and Roksolana Luciw, Anna Maksymowych, Anna Makuch, William Malenowski, Ulana Mazurkevich, Lidia Melnyk, Jurij Nakonechny, Evhen Novosad, Orysia Nowosivsky, Maria Panczak, Borys Pawliuk, Natalia Pazuniak, Nadya Petryk, Eugenia Podolak, Chrystina Prokopowich, Mykola Pryszlak, Osyp Roshka, Stefan Rozok, Wolodymyr Ryndich, Irene and Leonid Rudnytzky, Chrystia Senyk, Luba Siletska, John Siwak, Myron Soltys, Martha Tarnawska, Myrosia Woloshin, Stefan Yurchak, and Yaroslav Zalipsky.

Last but not least, hearty thanks belong to Christine Kulchyckyj, Richard Luyster, and my family (my wife, Mary, and my children, Ulita and Andrej) for the moral and physical assistance; and sincere thanks to my editor Erin Vosgien for her guidance in this project and to my proofreader Amanda Freeman.

INTRODUCTION

Philadelphia, the "Birthplace of America," is also known as the "Quaker City," the "Cradle of Liberty," the "City of Firsts," and the "City of Brotherly Love." Because of its historical and cultural achievements, many consider it to be the most prominent city in the United States. For this reason, Philadelphia was the site of the centennial exposition in 1876, the sesquicentennial exposition in 1926, and the bicentennial exposition in 1976. As fate would have it, it served as the center of Ukrainian life in the United States of America as well.

Geographically situated in the southeastern corner of Pennsylvania, about midway between New York City and Washington, D.C., Philadelphia is one of the main ports in the United States. Throughout its history, the metropolitan population has been approximately two million, with an additional two million people living in the beautiful, sprawling suburbs. It is a city replete with parks and museums.

Alexander Yaremko, sportscaster, writer, editor of *American-Ukrainian News*, president of Ukrainian American Citizens' Association (UACA), and a true Ukrainian American, referred to Philadelphia as the "Ukrainian Capital of America." This fact particularly is evident in the areas of religion, organization, education, culture, and athletics. It is well illustrated by the hundreds of buildings that Ukrainians possessed, with the aim of preserving Ukrainian identity, seeking recognition among other minorities of Philadelphia, and aspiring for an independent Ukraine. Since Ukrainian independence, economical and political assistance have continued to flow from the community in Philadelphia to the newly sovereign state.

Ukraine, located in the southeastern corner of Europe, north of the Black Sea, has a population of nearly 50 million people. Three times in the past 1,000 years sovereignty was gained, under various names. Invariably due to the attractiveness of natural resources and famously fertile lands, independence was short. In 1991, Ukrainian independence was once more proclaimed and recognized worldwide.

Ukrainians throughout the centuries had been referred to as Rusins, Ruthenians, Russnaks, Austrians, Russians, Poles, Hungarians, and the like. This historical fact alone exemplifies the Ukrainian identity crisis that most Ukrainian immigrants faced as they arrived in the United States in the 1870s and to Philadelphia en masse in the 1900s, with an inexact national identity. Regrettably it is still in the interest of some to continue this imprecise designation.

Better economic conditions offered by a system of free enterprise in the United States, greater freedom (notably in the areas of language and religion, which had been oppressed in the Polish and Russian parts of Ukraine), and greater opportunity of education were all significant factors in the influx of Ukrainians into the United States throughout the 125 years. These were the people, for the most part unlettered, except for the displaced persons (DPs) who arrived after World War II, whose calloused hands bore testimony of their work on the land. They were, including those who came after World War II, possessed of a certain gentility that was undoubtedly the fruit of a strong faith, which was the backbone of every family in their homeland. To this new land, these people brought their culture, a great love for their native tongue, and their religious faith and rite, as well as a strong attachment to their customs.

The first wave of immigrants left home for the United States of America in the 1880s to 1900s for economic reasons. More than one half returned with their earnings to their families. It was customary, before leaving for such an extended and perilous journey, to go to church and ask for the Blessed Mother's blessing and, oddly enough, to beg forgiveness for the inability to take care of the family. Another custom, one that is still practiced, is to bring a bit of native soil as a reminder of the homeland left behind. To them, America was a temporary haven. Still others, longing for the land of their birth, requested that at the time of their burial some Ukrainian soil be interred with them.

From 1910 to the 1930s, as conditions at home deteriorated during the war and famine years, Ukrainians, like so many other immigrant groups, were forced to remain abroad permanently. World War II and the ensuing cold war compelled the DPs to stay. Enforced Russification in Ukraine destroyed religion, culture, language, and the spirit of the people; this planned cultural genocide impelled Ukrainians to remain here permanently. Thus, throughout their history, the centers of Ukrainians in the United States initially began as missionary settlements. In time, however, they became permanent in order to maintain their Ukrainian heritage and became indefatigable spokesmen for their enslaved kin and Ukrainian statehood.

Since 1991, when Ukraine became independent, 20,000 Ukrainians have arrived in Philadelphia. They have come mostly for economic reasons. Today most are permanent residents unwilling to return, as the new Ukraine struggles with its fledgling democracy. Considering the hardships under which they lived, it is little wonder they desire to stay and pursue the "life, liberty, and happiness" principles on which the United States was born. What follows is the saga of Ukrainians in Philadelphia, in original photographs, admittedly incomplete though such a short story is inevitably destined to be so.

The first wave of Ukrainians came to Philadelphia between 1885 and 1905. This was the beginning of mass migrations, which led in time to great developments. On the one hand, in the old country there was talk of America as the land of milk and honey, which the village folk could hardly ignore. On the other hand, agents were looking for cheap labor for the expanding Industrial Revolution, as were representatives of large companies who were seeking strikebreakers. These two forces literally moved entire villages from the old country to the new. The newcomers were mainly young, strong men, healthy and ambitious. Because they did not know the local language and were unfamiliar with the new way of life they were handicapped, and as such they tended to live in common areas, feeling secure among their own in this strange land. And they built their churches; church was the savior, the link to the homeland.

One

SETTLING IN THE
CRADLE OF LIBERTY

*More than anything else, these people testify to the faith of their forefathers who came to this new
land more than 100 years ago with little more than love in their hearts and hope in their spirit.*

The Ukrainian immigrants arriving in Philadelphia between 1885 and 1905 faced different
hardships than those who migrated to rural areas. Adapting to a large metropolis was one
problem, language was another, and unknown ways of life was a third. Living in Ukrainian
neighborhoods solved some problems. The Polish, Slovak, and other Slavic immigrant groups
had similar concerns, as they too formed their own communities. The first community, composed
mostly of Ruthenians from Transcarpathia who came here in the late 1880s, was established in
southwestern Philadelphia in the area known as Point Breeze. In 1891, they built their church.
Other Ukrainian groups stayed in their chosen districts of the city and invited priests to serve
their spiritual needs, holding impromptu services in homes, as was the case of the Ukrainians
living in the area of Twenty-third and Callowhill Streets. At first, neither group wanted to
remain permanently in the United States. However, uncertainty in world politics, or perhaps
because they became surprisingly accustomed to the new way of life, made them realize that
other members of their village who were impoverished could benefit from living here. So they
sent letters home, encouraging others to join them. Most of these immigrants came from Skalat
Region in Ukraine. Soon after, Ukrainians from other regions under control of Austria-Hungary
began arriving.

Work in Philadelphia was plentiful. Jobs were available at Baldwin Locomotive, the sugar
refineries, the ironworks, or the docks. The few women who came worked mostly as domestics.
Since they were from various districts of Ukraine and spoke their own dialects, in time, the
language barrier among them created disharmony and forced them to separate from their only
Catholic church. Thus a second church, St. Michael's Greek Catholic Church on Buttonwood
Street, was formed where most of the Galicians from Western Ukraine lived. Both churches
catered to the Ukrainian immigrants until the arrival in 1907 of Bishop Soter Ortynsky, a
Ruthenian from Galicia who officially referred to himself as Ukrainian.

The advent of fraternal benefit societies, along with the various church organizations, and
the rise of ethnic newspapers incomparably contributed to keeping the Ukrainians together
in their established clusters. For their own safety and assurance in 1905, the first branch of
the Ukrainian National Association (UNA) Lubov, a fraternal benefit society, was organized.
Then came the literary reading room Prosvita, and soon after another branch of UNA was
organized in the Nicetown section of Philadelphia. Such was the meager start of the Ukrainian
community in Philadelphia.

Rev. John Wolansky was summoned in early 1884 by the Galician hierarchy to be pastor for the Ukrainians, at the time called Ruthenians, in Shenandoah, a part of the coal-mining region of Pennsylvania. Upon his arrival in the United States, he wanted to introduce himself to Archbishop Patrick Ryan of Philadelphia, the Latin Rite prelate within whose jurisdiction Shenandoah fell under. Reverend Wolansky and his wife spent the next three days in Philadelphia. On the first day, no one was able to see him. On the second day, he met with the vicar-general. On the third day, unable to meet with the archbishop, he and his wife left for Shenandoah without the hoped-for Episcopal blessing, remaining an enigma to the Latin Rite prelates solely because he was married. Married clergy has been the cornerstone of the Eastern Rite Ukrainian Catholic church; in the west, married clergy are forbidden. Thus Reverend Wolansky unknowingly began a controversy in the United States regarding married clergy. Because this issue had remained unresolved, it forced many Eastern Rite Catholics to leave their church to join the Orthodox or to form their own independent churches. As the seat of the Ukrainian Catholic Church in the United States was founded in Philadelphia, it has been the site of many demonstrations.

REV. J. WOLANSKI.
Drawing — *Shenandoah Herald.* October. 1886.

Paulina Hankewich (the daughter of a Greek Catholic priest) married Wolansky a year before his ordination in 1880. Wolansky received a special dispensation from the pope because he was ordained at the age of 23. Paulina was by his side throughout his pioneering missionary work in America and later in Brazil. Wolansky was the first Greek Catholic priest sent to the United States. When he filed his citizenship papers, he changed the spelling of his name from Wolanski to Wolansky. Paulina helped with the printing of the newspapers her husband began; she taught the parishioners who were unable to read and write; and she performed in the church drama clubs. Paulina died in Rio de Janero in 1891.

MRS. WOLANSKI.
Drawing — *Shenandoah Herald,* October, 1886

St. Michael's Greek Catholic Church on North Ninth Street (1895–1910), because of controversy, chose to be under the jurisdiction of the Russian Orthodox Church. As a result, Bishop Soter Ortynsky, in 1909, purchased a Presbyterian church on North Franklin Street and named it his Cathedral of the Immaculate Conception of the Blessed Virgin Mary. When Ukrainians from Galicia and the Carpathian Mountain regions started to immigrate en masse to Philadelphia in the 1890s, they completely ignored the Latin Rite hierarchy and started to form their own communities and brotherhoods. When sufficient numbers joined, they established their own Eastern Rite parishes, asking the hierarchy in Ukraine to send priests. This was the case of the first Ukrainians who founded a church at Twenty-fourth Street and Passyunk Avenue in the Point Breeze section of Philadelphia. As more arrived, they began to settle in various sections of Philadelphia. Some settled around Twenty-third and Callowhill Streets, others settled at Ninth and Buttonwood Streets. With time, sectionalism began to play an important part in the life of the Ukrainian immigrant. When a sufficient number of immigrants from a particular village in the old country arrived, they formed a close community, perpetuating their own dialect and their local mores and customs and eventually breaking away from the already formed settlements and starting their own centers. A church edifice was essential. Thus the St. Michael's Society was formed, and in a short time, St. Michael's Greek Catholic Church became the Ukrainian stronghold in Philadelphia. St. Michael's Society was founded in September 1895, with the purpose of organizing a parish on Ninth Street. When Bishop Ortynsky arrived in 1907, the need for a cathedral became acute. St. Michael's Society declined to sign over its church. A court challenge followed that was so protracted that Bishop Ortynsky purchased a Protestant church and made it his cathedral. From 1903 to 1915, the St. Michael's Society was affiliated with the UNA; afterward they joined the Providence Association of Ukrainian Catholics.

The UACA Hall on North Franklin Street in the Northern Liberties section served many purposes. In 1917, this troupe rehearsing for an upcoming performance was immortalized. They are, from left to right, Mychajlo Pelensky, Petro Zybrytsky, three unidentified, Stefan Demkiw, Anastasia Rybakova, Ilko Zatonskyj, Maria Chernykhivska, Hryhoryj Chernykhivsky, and Mychajlo Rybak.

Members of the Prosvita reading room in 1907 are, from left to right, (seated, first row) Stefan Demkiw, Mychajlo Polak, Ivan Krechkovsky, and Mykola Rosolovich; (second row) Ivan Demkiw, Anna Rosolovich, Pelagia Polak, Maria Krechkovska, Petro Krechkovsky, and Antin Kluchnyk; (third row) Mykola Sitnytskyj, Ivan Dushka, Mychajlo Vyshyvaniuk, and Mychajlo Dovbenko.

Two

BROTHERLY LOVE
IN ACTION

They needed a champion who could speak their language, know their ways,
and could encourage and advise them in a strange land.
—Paul Dubas, Ukrainian pioneer, chronicler, activist, dentist.

Philadelphia boasted two branches of the UNA, a reading room, and two churches, each with its own choir, before the arrival of Bishop Soter Ortynsky in 1907. Shortly after his arrival, he became a living example to the Ukrainians with his dynamic personality, leadership qualities, knowledge of English as well as other languages, and his consequent naturalization. In Philadelphia, Bishop Ortynsky organized a Ukrainian center on Franklin Street near the site of the future cathedral. By 1909, the Horozhansky Klub, later known as the UACA, was founded, and in 1910, Bishop Ortynsky became an honorary member.

The UACA is the oldest existing Ukrainian club in North America. In its first 60 years, it was the center of Ukrainian life in Philadelphia. The UACA has a rich history and served as the founding place of most present-day Ukrainian organizations. Some of the more prominent ones founded on North Franklin Street were the Ukrainian Savings and Loan Association, the Ukrainian American Veterans Organization, the Central Ukrainian American Committee of Philadelphia, the Ukrainian Congress Committee of America, the Ukrainian National Women's League of America, the United Ukrainian American Clubs of Philadelphia, the United Ukrainian American Relief Committee, the Ukrainian Heritage School, the Ukrainian Drama Club, and several choirs. For decades, the UACA was also the social club of Ukrainian Americans in Philadelphia, hosting conventions, conferences, meetings, performances, dances, sporting, and scholastic events. Today it is nestled between Ascension Manor, the two eight-story buildings for retirees managed by the Ukrainian Metropolitan See on the north, and the new $4 million Ukrainian Catholic Cathedral and the Archieparchy headquarter complex, incorporating the rectory, the church hall, the old school (converted to the Treasury of Faith Archieparchial Museum), and a religious goods store, to the south. The UACA is situated on two acres of land purchased from the Philadelphia Redevelopment Authority and is developing a picnic ground and a multipurpose sports field.

It was during these years that Ukrainians established themselves a well-deserved reputation as hardworking, enterprising, and moral people. Because of this reputation, the City of Philadelphia permitted three blocks on North Franklin Street, between Girard Avenue and Parish Street, to become a Ukrainian center with far-reaching goals. Some of them were achieved, others are being developed, and still others are just in the planning stages.

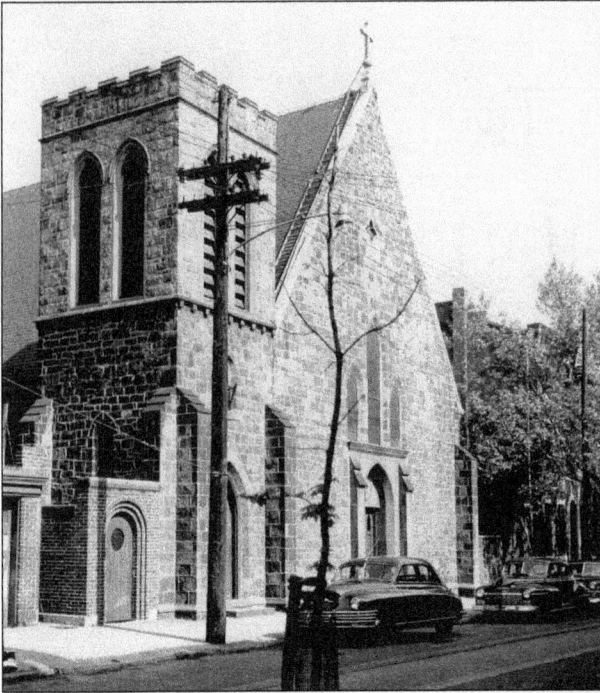

The Ukrainian Catholic Cathedral of the Immaculate Conception on North Franklin Street building was purchased in 1909 by Bishop Soter Ortynsky and was in use until a new cathedral building was completed in 1966. Metropolitan Andrej Sheptytsky officiated at the solemn blessing of the cathedral in October 1910. This was the first visit of the metropolitan to the United States.

The buildings for the motherhouse and orphanage of the Sisters of St. Basil the Great Sacred Heart Province in the United States were purchased in 1911 by Bishop Ortynsky and given to the sisters for their mission. The corner building was the monastery. The building to the right was used for the orphans. The sisters established a day school, a sewing center for liturgical vestments, and in 1917, began publishing the monthly *Missionary*. The complex was expanded when additional classrooms were needed. The school was started in 1925, in a three-story, 13-room apartment house at the corner of Parrish and Franklin Streets.

Seen here is the 10th convention of UNA in Philadelphia in 1908, and Bishop Ortynsky, an honorary member, is seated in the first row (center). The next convention, held in Cleveland in 1910, caused internal conflict due to a new designation, no longer Ruthenian but Greek Catholic after considerable pressure from Ortynsky. In time, this led to a split in UNA, with one section called the Ukrainian Workingmen's Association and the other the Association of Ruthenian Greek Catholic Church Brotherhoods "Christian Love" in America. Later it became known as the Providence Association of Ukrainian Catholics (Providence), established by Ortynsky.

The Myr Society, established in 1912, was incorporated into Branch No. 324 of UNA in 1916, by the Ukrainian League of Philadelphia at Twenty-third and Brown Streets in the Fairmount section. They purchased a building in 1918 to be used for an evening school, Ukrainian League of Philadelphia business, and a club room in the basement. During the two world wars, UNA assumed leadership in contributing toward the war effort, rallying the Ukrainian people to support government drives such as aiding the American Red Cross and purchasing war bonds.

On February 12, 1911, Theodozia Goy, 20 years old, born in the village of Plaskiwci, married Stefan Zaharachuk, 26 years old, from the village of Terpylivka. Both villages were in Western Ukraine (at that time a part of the Austro-Hungarian Empire). Goy's brother and Zaharachuk served in the Austrian army from 1903 to 1907. Upon Zaharachuk's arrival in the United States, a courtship that had started by mail ended in marriage at the Ukrainian Catholic Cathedral of the Immaculate Conception.

This group photograph was taken in front of the church hall where many parish activities took place. In the second row are, from left to right, starting at the third person, Peter Gramiak, Prokip Mosiondz, Rev. Roman Krupa, Michael Orlak, and Wasyl Pohorylo, pioneers of the parish. St. Josaphat's Branch No. 14 of Providence in Frankford was established in 1913.

One of the oldest branches of Providence, established in 1915, is pictured in the courtyard of the orphanage. It was also the earliest to be disbanded due to the steady influx of new immigrants who organized branches in their local neighborhoods.

The literary society, honoring Ivan Franko, was part of UNA Branch No. 83. Members are in the courtyard of the orphanage with a portrait of Franko in the center. Franko was a Ukrainian scholar, poet, and novelist.

Branch No. 120 of Providence was made up of veterans of the Ukrainian Sichovy Striltsi. They formed the honor guard at the funeral of Bishop Soter Ortynsky in 1916. This photograph is from 1920.

Members of the UACA pose with the honorary member Bishop Ortynsky shortly before his death in 1916. Bishop Ortynsky is seated in the second row, eighth from the right.

Katherine Rosolovich debuts her piano mastery during Ukrainian Day festivities on October 5, 1915. Her career as a soloist and accompanist extended from 1915 to 1937.

St. Michael the Archangel, Branch No. 7 of Providence in 1917, poses with the insignia of the branch. Rev. Maxim Kinash is in the second row, fifth from the left. After the death of Bishop Ortynsky, some members from St. Michael's Greek Catholic Church joined the cathedral branch. This photograph was taken in the courtyard of the orphanage with the convent seen on the left.

Seen here is the Missionary School of St. Paul the Apostle in 1917. The school was organized in 1915 and mainly included orphans who belonged to St. Andrew's School that Bishop Soter Ortynsky established in 1911. The portrait is of Ortynsky. The adults seated in the middle of the second row are, Rev. Zachary Orun (rector), Maxim Kinash (pastor), and Andrew Gella (choir director). St. Paul's later became a Minor Seminary.

St. Michael's Choir was under the direction of Ivan Krychkowsky from 1905 to 1909; later it joined the cathedral in 1909 to form the Cathedral Choir. The first director of this choir was Wasyl Kociubinsky (second row, fifth from left); Rev. Maxim Kinash and Eugene Yakubovich are next to him.

Members of this popular 1918 dance quartet are, from left to right, ? Hrebeniak, Anastasia Rybak (who also performed in the theater), Mychajlo Rybak (kneeling in front), and Wolodymyr Kowal (who was the first Ukrainian American physician in Philadelphia).

Seen with students of the first Ukrainian evening school in 1917 are Rev. Maxim Kinash (center), pastor of the cathedral and a popular speaker at numerous concerts between 1915 and 1924, and Andrew Gela (first row, second from right), cantor and director of the cathedral choir.

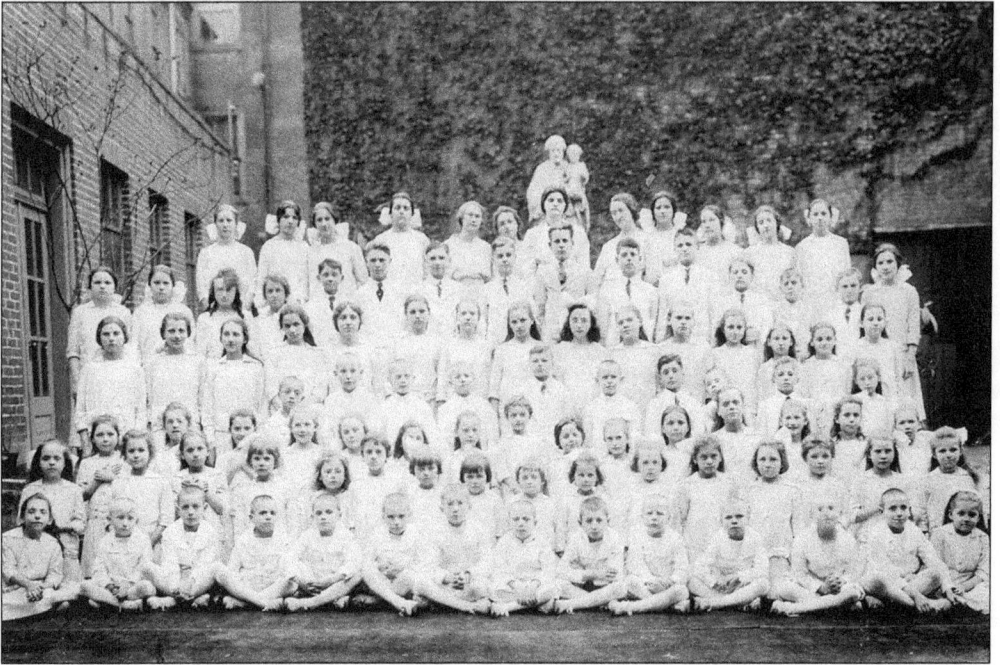

Orphans posed in the courtyard of St. Basil's in 1918, in front of the statue of St. Joseph. The statue of St. Joseph, a favorite saint of Mother Superior, was erected because the school began as St. Joseph's School. The name was later changed so as not to be confused with other St. Joseph's Schools. On the back left is the multipurpose hall, and in the rear is the boys' dormitory.

America, the first Ukrainian Catholic daily newspaper outside of Ukraine, was started in New Britain, Connecticut, in 1912. It transferred to Philadelphia in 1914 and was printed at the orphanage print house by the Sisters of St. Basil the Great; after a while, Providence purchased a printing press. Throughout its 95-year history, it was published daily, thrice weekly, or weekly. Seen here are, from left to right, (first row) Paul Kiryluk (manager), Anthony Curkowsky (editor), Evhen Yakubovich, and Wasyl Kostecky; (second row) Alexander Dzmelyk, Wasyl Semotiak, and David Ostiak.

By 1911, the cathedral on Franklin Street established many organizations for both men and women. The faithful displayed their insignias during processions in church and on public occasions. This unidentified member of the Apostleship of Prayer chose to have her picture taken possibly to send home to family, as was customary at that time. The Apostleship of Prayer was organized in every parish for the purpose of spreading the glory of God and for the salvation of their souls. They sponsored various social affairs with the proceeds going for the needs of the church.

Seated in the center are, from left to right, Wasyl Kociubinsky, Rev. Maxim Kinash, and Andrew Gella (choir director), with members of the 1918 Ukrainian Catholic Cathedral Choir in their national dress. They also performed at various cultural affairs with national themes.

St. Josaphat's Ukrainian Catholic Church held its initial First Holy Communion in 1918; pictured in the center is Rev. Wolodymyr Petriwsky, the pastor.

Photographed in 1919 are the girls and Sisters of St. Basil's Orphanage in the courtyard, dressed in the clothing they tailored.

A typical play staged at the UACA Hall is seen in this photograph. Many of the plays had themes of the old country, reminding the immigrants of home. The stage and hall were completely refurbished in 1922.

Metropolitan Andrej Sheptytsky of Lviv is seen here surrounded by the orphans and Sisters of St. Basil the Great on the occasion of his visit to Philadelphia in 1922.

ПОЗИЧКА НАЦІОНАЛЬНОЇ ОБОРОНИ

ДЛЯ ЗДОБУТТЯ І ЗАКРІПЛЕННЯ НЕЗАЛЕЖНОСТИ ГАЛИЦЬКОЇ ДЕРЖАВИ.

СЕРІЯ: 001

№ 0480

НА

ПЯТЬ АМЕРИКАНСЬКИХ ДОЛЯРІВ

які зложив ...... *Роман Карбівник* ......

замешкалий в ...... *Philadelphia Pa.* ......

На основі цеї тимчасової посвідки одержить оказатель її довжний запис десятьлітної, уморимої 6%-ової Позички Національної Оборони згідно з рішенням Президента Галицької Української Національної Ради з дня 21. червня 1921 року, ч. 368/През. Д.

Опроцентування і сплата цеї позички, яку виготовлено частками по серіям, відбувається по постановам, оголошеним в проспек-ті з дня 23. червня 1921 року.

Відень дня 23. червня 1921 року.

За Фінансову Комісію:

УРЯД ДИПЛЬОМАТИЧНОГО ПРЕДСТАВНИЦТВА
ЗАХ. УКР. (ГАЛИЦЬКОЇ) НАРОДНОЇ РЕПУБЛИКИ В АМЕРИЦІ

Відділ II. (фінансово-торговельний)

Виставлено в Вашінгтоні дня ...... 19. 9. 1921. ......

За Контрольну Комісію:

In the years following Ukrainian independence in 1918 and 1919, the government of Ukraine issued national bonds to mature in 10 years at six percent interest. Many immigrants supported this national defense effort. In 1921, Roman Karbiwnyk, a prominent Ukrainian Philadelphian, purchased this $5 bond.

The Sitch Society was organized following World War I to economically and physically help Ukraine gain independence. It supported a pro-hetman (Cossack) type of government, and its training resembled that of the Cossacks. In Philadelphia, the society owned a building at Brown and Franklin Streets as well as several branches throughout the city. Pictured is Branch No. 1 of the Sitch Society.

Participants at a Ukrainian veterans' memorial service in 1923 placed a wreath at the Tomb of the Unknown Soldier; seen here are, from left to right, Sophia Rosolovich, Katherine Rosolovich, Betty Kinash, and Olha Wyshywaniuk.

This building was originally purchased by UACA in 1925 and used as a hall and club room. Throughout its 98 illustrious years, the UACA has accomplished numerous achievements. During this time, it never faltered from American principles while perpetuating a Ukrainian way of life away from the homeland for its members. The leadership sponsored an array of activities from educational to athletic. It could easily be called the Ukrainian hub, located just one block from the cathedral on North Franklin Street.

St. Josaphat's Ukrainian Catholic Church is the second church, with the rectory on the left and hall on Tacony Street where social activities of the parish occurred in the 1950s and 1960s before a new hall was built. Ukrainians settled Frankford at the beginning of the 20th century. By 1916, they purchased a Methodist church and converted it for their use. The Sichovy Striltsi Society was established in 1916, and an orchestra was formed under the supervision of Mychajlo Bahlay; he later initiated the church choir. In 1951, a new church and later a school were built by Rev. Myroslav Charyna. The interior of the church was decorated in the Ukrainian style by Petro Andrusiw.

St. Josaphat's Ukrainian Catholic Church Shashkewych Choir was organized in 1927. In the middle are, from left to right, Paul Bahlay, Rev. Roman Krupa, and Michael Grolsko.

Three

UKRAINIAN LIFESTYLES

Through the untiring zeal and benevolent efforts of this generation, the Old Country would live forever in the hearts and minds of the American children of Ukrainian descent.
—Chronicles of St. Basil's School

From 1917, Ukrainian life mainly centered on the Ukrainian Catholic Church and the sports clubs. In the 1920s, the Orthodox and Baptist churches came into existence, and the community expanded. This phenomenon continued until the 1990s, when attention was shifted toward the newly acquired Ukrainian Educational and Cultural Center (UECC), which became the nucleus housing many of the clubs and organizations that existed in Philadelphia.

The UACA was the most influential club due to its central location; in time, however, other clubs came into existence, offering similar amenities: a hall, a bar, meeting rooms, and even some indoor sports facilities. In 1944, seven clubs formed the United Ukrainian American Clubs of Philadelphia, and by 1946, they published a newspaper. The seven clubs that joined were the Ukrainian League of Nicetown on Rowan Street; the Ukrainian League of Philadelphia on Brown Street; the Ukrainian League of Philadelphia on Lawrence Street; the Ukrainian American League of Frankford on Wakeling Street; the Progressive American Club on Germantown Avenue; and the Ukrainian American Citizens League of South Philadelphia on American Street.

After World War I, Ukraine's western lands, once part of Austria-Hungary, were given to Poland as war compensation and the eastern lands became part of the emerging Soviet Union, so the Ukrainians in Philadelphia had no choice but to remain. With their families under foreign rule, they became politically active. The social clubs in their respective districts of Philadelphia became centers of antisocialism, anticommunism, and antiforeign rule. In this age of the 1920s and 1930s, protest demonstrations were plentiful. Even theatrical performances were reminders of the agony in the motherland. Just as pro-Americanism flourished during the Great War with war bonds being the main source of support, so too did antiforeign dominance of Ukraine become the focal point of resentment. These turbulent foreign events, along with the coming Great Depression, made the Ukrainian American clubs a focal point for discussions and focused attention on sports. Simultaneously an increase in religious fervor was born, which intensified with the outbreak of World War II.

During these decades, some Ukrainians were convinced that this land, the Ukrainian Soviet Socialist Republic, was a Soviet, but independent, nation. Among the nationalists, they were referred to as leftists, socialists, and communists. Nevertheless, they had their own progressive lodges, establishing their own small communities; most belonged to the Orthodox-Muscovite church or to no church at all. Their ideology was pro-Moscow, therefore as Ukrainians they chose not to participate in the Ukrainian community at large.

In 1924, Bishop Constantine Bohachevsky became the exarch of the Ukrainian Catholic Church in the United States. For more than 35 years, he worked unceasingly to strengthen the church's organizational structure. Among his many achievements was the establishment of a diocesan school system that included the Minor Seminary, evening, and parochial schools. The Holy See elevated the exarchate of Philadelphia to a metropolitan see on August 12, 1958, naming Bishop Bohachevsky the archbishop metropolitan. By January 6, 1961, when he died, Philadelphia had come of age.

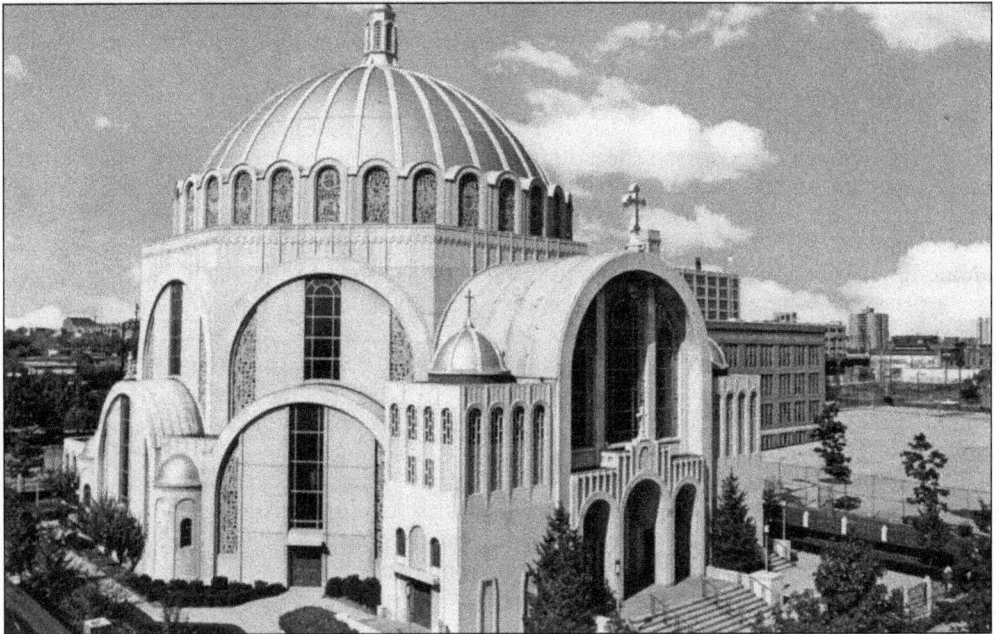

The new Cathedral of the Immaculate Conception, mother church of the Ukrainian Catholic Metropolitan Province in the United States, was built in 1966. This edifice replaced the old cathedral. The new cathedral reflects the beauty and richness of the religious and cultural heritage of the Ukrainian people. It hosted many dignitaries, including Pope John Paul II and Patriarch Josyf Slipyj.

Ioan Teodorovych, metropolitan of the Ukrainian Orthodox Church, came to the United States at the request of Orthodox Ukrainians in North America and at the behest of the All-Ukrainian Orthodox Church Council in 1924. He settled in Philadelphia and chose St. Vladimir Ukrainian Orthodox Church, presently on North Fifth Street, for his cathedral. Teodorovych dedicated his life to uniting the two main factions of the Ukrainian Orthodox Church, leaving behind a collection of popular theological works, meditations, and fiction.

St. Vladimir Ukrainian Orthodox Cathedral on North Fifth Street began in 1925 as St. Andrew's Ukrainian Orthodox Church. In 1930, a suitable church located at the corner of Germantown Avenue and Berk Street was purchased. Throughout the decades, it boasted of a Ukrainian school and a professional choir under the direction of Peter Kurylenko and Rev. John Sawchuk. In 1965, the parish moved to the North Fifth Street location, where it continued to spiritually serve the Orthodox Ukrainians as a cathedral until 2000.

The Ukrainian club in the Society Hill section began an evening school. The initiators are, from left to right, (first row) Gregory Lysiuk, Rev. Paul Procko (pastor of the cathedral), Theodore Hrycay, and Julia Zwolinska (teacher at the South Philadelphia Ukrainian school); (second row) two unidentified men.

The UACA Women's Auxiliary began in 1929 with the intention of finding much-needed funds for the UACA. At first, it functioned with the men's association, but in time, it staged its own picnics, commemorative days, and other celebrations. This photograph was taken in 1943.

The home office of the Providence Association of Ukrainian Catholics in America is on Franklin Street. On the left are the offices of the newspaper *America*; on the right is the remodeled building housing the printing press, conference rooms, and the main office of the Providence Association of Ukrainian Catholics. This group is a fraternal benefit organization founded by the first Ukrainian Catholic Bishop in the United States, Soter Ortynsky, in 1912 in Philadelphia. As a fraternal benefit organization, it was established to enable its members to save for their own future, their children's education and welfare, and insurance coverage in case of death. The Providence Association of Ukrainian Catholics is also a civic organization based on Catholic principles. Its aims and purposes are to spread and strengthen spiritual life among Ukrainian Americans in the United States, so that they continue to be faithful to the Ukrainian Catholic Church and nation and to strengthen national awareness among Ukrainian Americans in the United States, so they will become knowledgeable citizens. In addition to the aforementioned aims, it is responsible in conducting various cultural and community works. Throughout its illustrious history, its printing house produced over 100 major publications (in Ukrainian and in English) and published several diverse newspapers, pamphlets, and other printing materials. It also participated in religious activities as the Marianist and Eucharistic Congresses, installations of bishops and metropolitans, and other significant community affairs. Over 14 branches existed in Philadelphia alone, donating money for various religious and patriotic causes.

The Ukrainian club at Twenty-third and Brown Streets is the home of the Ukrainian League of Philadelphia, founded in 1916, by UNA Branch No. 324, Myr. Its first home was on Fairmount Avenue, where it started an evening school, nursery school, and a club. Later it formed the Ukrainian Athletic Association, a theater and drama club, and choirs. By the time of World War II, it also set up a library. After World War II, it hosted Moloda Prosvita.

The Taras Shevchenko Dramatic Club and Choir from the Fairmount section's Ukrainian community is seen in 1930; Dmytro Stetsyk, the director, organized the group in 1925. Its repertoire included *Beztalanna*, *Bat'kova Kazka*, *Uchytyl*, *Ukradzhene Schastya*, and many more. Taras Shevchenko is the bard of Ukraine.

The Cossack Choir is seen here in 1937, under the direction of Stefan Sawchuk, who is standing sideways on the left. The choir, a program of UACA, also performed as a dance troupe.

The first Women's Auxiliary of Strilecka Hromada was organized in 1930. Women play a major role in Ukrainian social and cultural life and so formed auxiliary branches of organizations that the men had formed.

Girls of Ukrainian descent are shown in the traditional garb of their forefathers as they march down the Benjamin Franklin Parkway in a parade protesting Polish oppression in East Galicia. In the background is one of the many protest signs that the marchers carried. This image is from the *Philadelphia Record* of December 1, 1930.

1732　1932

UKRAINIAN BICENTENNIAL COMMITTEE

in

TRIBUTE

to

WASHINGTON

presents

ALEXANDER KOSHETZ

and his

UKRAINIAN CHORUS

"—most amazing and beautiful singing heard in the memory of a middle aged man."

(New York Evening Sun.)

also

VASILE AVRAMENKO

and his

UKRAINIAN FOLK BALLET

"—a most inspired pageant of historical and festive dances." (Pittsburgh Sun-Telegraph.)

AMERICAN ACADEMY OF MUSIC,

BROAD & LOCUST STREETS,　　PHILADELPHIA, PA.

FRIDAY, MAY 6th, 1932,

at 8.15 P. M.

Tickets: $1.00 to $3.00.

The Ukrainian community paid homage to George Washington's bicentennial in 1932 with a concert by the internationally renowned Alexander Koshetz Choir and Vasyl Avramenko's Folk Ballet School. Entertainment and education were offered by the music, and ballet for the program was made up entirely of folk music written for the occasion. The folklore presentation was of Ukraine rising with its unmatched wealth of youthful, untouched vitality.

Danylo Skoropadsky, son of Hetman Pavlo Skoropadsky, head of the free Ukrainian nation from 1918 to 1919, traveled extensively throughout the United States during 1937 and 1938 to meet hetman supporters. In 1937, students of St. Basil's Academy welcomed him with a concert held in his honor.

This sign on one of the entrances to Philadelphia City Hall welcomes the 1938 convention of the Ukrainian Catholic Youth League (UCYL). The UCYL was founded in 1933. This organization, with the ideals of serving God and country, participated in parish life. It donated money for many causes. The goal was to prepare youth to continue the noble work begun by their parents in their new homeland. For this purpose, the UCYL sponsored dances and sporting events, held conventions, published newsletters, set up cultural trips, and sponsored annual Christmas parties for orphans.

The Brotherhood of All Saints was organized in 1920 by Rev. Wolodymyr Dowhovich with the goal of uniting all priests and cantors, as well as members of the board of directors of Providence. This branch was not fixed to one locality, and many members were leaders in other organizations in Philadelphia; for example, in the 1920s, Ivan Moroz, Evhen Yakubovich, Michael Klymko, and Wolodymyr Yaskevich were members. Later Michael Darmopray, Wolodymyr Lotocky, Osyp Stojkevych, and Wolodymyr Doroshenko belonged and were benefactors for the new cathedral.

The Ukrainian American group Dramatic Circle of Lesia Ukrainka was organized under the auspices of Soyuz Ukrainok in 1938. This group in 1942 was under the direction of Dmytro Pasichnyk (sixth from left, second row). Lesia Ukrainka is the lyric poetess of Ukraine much favored by Ukrainian Americans.

St. Andrew's Ukrainian Catholic parish was established in 1943 for Ukrainians living in the Society Hill section, as well as for those living in South Philadelphia. The new church was built in 1952 on Pine Street. The Society Hill section is composed of the old historic city and its immediate surroundings. In the beginning there was a social club. After World War II, it became desirable to live in the suburbs and many people left the area. With the dwindling number of parishioners, the church was eventually closed. It was sold in the past few years.

The Executive Board of Providence in 1942 was, from left to right, (first row) Rev. Anthony Borsa, Rev. Walter Bilinsky, and Ivan Rosolowych; (second row) Peter Kyraliuk (manager), Eugene Rohach, Bohdan Katamaj (editor), and Antin Curkowsky (editor).

Several members of the Ukrainian Catholic Cathedral Choir in traditional Ukrainian dress are preparing *pysanky* for Easter. The choir members are Helen Nahirny, Ann Matkowska, Pearl Bega, Mary Gudera, and Ann Chemeny. *Pysanky* writing is an ancient art form handed down from mother to daughter. Although the photograph is undated, it could be contemporary.

Souvenir Program

Eight Annual Contest
for the title of

Miss Ukraine 1942
sponsored by

The Ukrainian Radio Program

SATURDAY EVENING, MAY 2nd, 1942
UKRAINIAN HALL
849 North Franklin Street,   Philadelphia, Pa.

This is a souvenir program from the annual Miss Ukraine contest held in 1942. This program was sponsored by Theodore Swystun's radio program and continued into the 1950s.

IN MEMORY

LET US NOT FORGET - BUT *Remember Pearl Harbor*
AND THOSE WHO DIED FOR LIBERTY

ANTHONY BILYI

Born in Philadelphia, Pa , June 16, 1921

Educated in Phila. Public Schools · Jefferson, Kearney, Central High and
Benjamin Franklin High School.
Assistant Director and First President of Phila. Cadet Band
1st Member of the following organizations to be killed at Pearl Harbor :
American Coast Patrol, Aqua String Band, Northern Liberty Cadet Band
Y. M. C. A. Neighborhood Club, Evening Bulletin Carrier, and the first boy from
Central Historical Philadelphia to lose his life while serving his country.

ANTHONY BILYI

Enlisted in U. S. Navy, Oct. 16, 1940
Served on the U. S. S. SHAW 373

Died in Defense of his Country
DECEMBER 7, 1941 at PEARL HARBOR

★ HONOR ROLL ★

U. S. NAVY	U. S. ARMY	U. S. MARINES
★ Anthony Bilyi	Jack Tinsman	Alfred R. Crossley
Robert Camerdese	Sgt. Anthony Camerdese	John Balanovich
Harry Gregorczyn	John Parhat	Wm. Merdith
Matthew Morroz	Frank Domanski	
Samuel Kowal	Eddie Kurtz	**U. S. ARMY**
John Hasiak	Wm. Kurtas	Joseph Samyon
John Moknatch	Hasting Lamb	Joseph Luther
Jess Cramer	Alex. Prochorenko	Thomas Seward
Thomas Rice	Paul C. Halsey	Frank Hoffman
Michael Nawalany	Amandus Spielberger	Edward Stec
Joseph Fallon	Ludwig Orchowiereski	Morris Levine
Sol Schur	Edward Sparks	G. Kushina
Joseph Coulter	Frank Sparks	Bernard Learner
Peter Kruvczuk	Benjamin Galaski	Alfred Masterpleto
Wm. Weinmuller	Walter Kurko	Andrew Koshinski
John Halchuk	Wm. Phillips	Peter Kurko
Gilbert Spruance	Walter Bernackie	Charles Carney
Wm. Renner	Walter Fallon	Elmer H. McCusker,
Harry Crammer	John Sevick	R. A. F.

First Memorial Service held Sunday, Feb. 22, 1942. 3 P. M., Central Branch, Y. M. C. A., 1421 Arch St., Phila., Pa.

Auspices of American Coast Patrol, Inc., Phila.

M. Martain Renner, Nat'l Com.   Christie Urback, Nat'l Radio Staff   Lt. Chas. H. Angelo, Nat'l Engineer Staff
J. Liming, Nat'l Asst. Com.   Edgar C. Clymer, State Com., Pa.   Y. M. C. A. Services in charge of A. O. Becker
Parade in charge of Daniel A. Hancock, Marshall Service Officer, A. M. Forsthoffer Post 389, V. F. W.

Anthony Bilyi died at Pearl Harbor. He was the first young man from historical central Philadelphia to lose his life while serving his country. The Ukrainian American Veterans Post No. 1 at the UACA was named in his memory.

In 1946, the Ukrainian League of Philadelphia in the Fairmount section organized the John Karbowsky Post No. 2 of the Ukrainian American Veterans. This post, as all the others, participated in Memorial Day services, decorating and visiting the graves of Ukrainian American veterans. Peter Mosiondz Jr., a member of this post, also served in Vietnam. In 1958, a Ladies Auxiliary of Post No. 2 was formed.

The UACA Club team is seen during the 1945–1946 season. They are, from left to right, (first row) Joseph Berezowsky, Joseph Kapral, Alexander Hrynkow, Steven Senkow, and Paul Panasosky; (second row) Theodore Bochey, Jaroslav Juzwiak (coach for 10 years), Joseph Pistun, Specks Bukata (perennial captain), and Alexander Demnianyk; (third row) John Nagurney, Joseph Zurybida, George Slobogin, Melanie Olesh, Dietric Slobogin, Stephen Senkow, and William Juzwiak. Of the 500 games they played, about 100 were with other Ukrainian teams.

Mothers of the young men and women who served in the armed forces during World War II gathered for the dedication of the service flag at the Ukrainian Catholic Cathedral of the Immaculate Conception on Franklin Street in 1942.

Honorary members of the UACA pose in 1943. They are, from left to right, (first row) Stephen Stogryn, Mychajlo Wyshywaniuk, John Borosiewicz, George Szagala, and John Soroka; (second row) Anthony Harasym, Michael Rehulyk, John Pelensky, Mykyta Buryj, and Ivan Chawliuk.

Refugees in Austria organized the Vatra, a Ukrainian male chorus, in 1946. They toured Europe from 1946 to 1951, under the direction of Lev Turkevych. In order to save the group, 72 affidavits were issued, mostly from members of the Ukrainian League of Philadelphia, especially Osyp Bakaj. They were submitted to the United Ukrainian American Relief Committee (UUARC) to facilitate entry into the United States. When the choir arrived, it performed at the Ukrainian League of Philadelphia's hall in Philadelphia. Unable to get sponsorship for the entire group, some members joined Kobzar, a choir under the direction of Antin Rudnytsky.

November 1 is the Annual Day of Remembrance for the soldiers who died in the struggle for the liberation of Ukraine. Pictured is such a ceremony at St. Mary's Ukrainian Catholic Cemetery in Fox Chase.

The annual pilgrimages to the Grotto of the Mother of God on the campus of the Sisters of St. Basil the Great in Fox Chase began in the 1940s. This pilgrimage on Mother's Day brought together alumni as well as students of St. Basil's Academy and Manor Junior College, their family, friends, and the Ukrainian community from near and far.

According to Ukrainian spiritual heritage, water is blessed on the Feast of Theophany. In the old cathedral the blessing was held in the courtyard with the faithful gathered at the foot of a cross made of ice (on the left).

The first Ukrainian Savings and Loan Association was organized and incorporated in Philadelphia in 1918. During World War II, the Ukrainian Savings and Loan Association sold Liberty Bonds and purchased the Liberty Ships *Bishop Ortynsky* and *Father Honcharenko*. After World War II, with the arrival of the DPs, they helped in resettlement, home construction, and the opening of businesses. The Ukrainian Savings and Loan Association takes an active part in the Ukrainian community life.

In the early 1950s, parishioners of St. Nicholas Ukrainian Catholic Church participate in the ancient ritual of having traditional foods blessed for Easter by Rev. Ivan Lebedowych.

Four

UKRAINIAN RENAISSANCE IN PHILADELPHIA

We can be good Ukrainians without knowing all of the whys and wherefores and correct grammar,
but we can be better Ukrainians and Americans if we do know.
—*Our Life*, 1949

The war years took their toll on the Ukrainians living in Philadelphia. The boys went to war, and the girls went to work. A vacuum developed in the sociocultural life of the permanent immigrants. Newspapers folded, the Ukrainian Cultural Center slowly ceased its operation, and the function of the clubs disintegrated to such a degree that they joined hands in order to survive. Only religious life took an upward swing, mostly because of personal and global tragedies.

Then in 1947, the DPs began arriving. They came by the thousands, many of whom landed and stayed in Philadelphia. At first, it looked as if the old immigrants and the new immigrants were going to join hands, but it did not happen. The DPs were of a different stock; this so-called "Ukrainian political immigration" was just that. These new Ukrainians had been forcibly removed from their land during World War II. Most of them resettled in DP camps in West Germany and Austria; others managed to survive on their own in larger cities scattered throughout western Europe. In these camps (1945–1950), as in the cities, they formed societies, schools, religious institutions, political parties, benefit organizations, the whole array of community life.

With their new freedom, they were not about to assimilate under any conditions. They came to Philadelphia with practically nothing but the firm hope that their stay would be very short. Wholeheartedly they believed that Ukraine would be free within 5 to 15 years, and then they could return home. Therefore their idea of a temporary community life in the United States was diametrically opposed to the existing one. As a result, throughout the 1950s, parallel Ukrainian societies emerged in Philadelphia. On the one hand, the old immigrants had their established societies that were pro-Ukrainian, pro-Russian, or pro-Soviet Ukraine. On the other hand, the new immigrants, with their temporary Ukrainian societies, were anti-Russian, anti-Soviet, and anti-Polish. They established their own schools, scientific societies, artistic ensembles, children's nurseries, youth organizations, and other professional institutions with very little regard for the American way of life. All their efforts were focused on preserving their Ukrainian heritage.

In time, the new immigrants chose a different road. They did not remain in the North Franklin Street neighborhood as the old immigrants had hoped. They moved rather quickly, primarily north and northeast but also southwest of Franklin Street and some even out of state. This became evident by the number of new churches built in diverse sections of Philadelphia.

The First Ukrainian Evangelical-Baptist Church on Large Street was bought in 1973, when the congregation moved from the First Baptist Church on Seventh Street and the House of Prayer on Erie Avenue. The first group came because of persecution. The second group came because of economic conditions and compulsory military service in Europe. The third group came to better their lives. This congregation is composed of the post–World War II immigrants and the latest wave of immigrants who came over in the 1990s.

Christ the King Ukrainian Catholic Church on Cayuga Street in the Nicetown section was established in 1949 by the post–World War II immigrants. The complex included a rectory (left of church), a parish hall (a former protestant church), and a library, located on the corner of Sixteenth and Cayuga Streets. The parish also owned several other buildings. They were used in the 1950s and 1960s to house the Ukrainian Saturday school Ridna Shkola. Later the school rented different public schools, making them available to house additional priests.

St. Nicholas Ukrainian Catholic Church at Twenty-fourth and Poplar Streets is seen here as it is today. A church was bought in 1944, along with a building for a rectory. In 1951, the school was built. A new church was started in the 1960s. The Ukrainians of the Fairmount section already founded Moloda Prosvita by 1912, and by 1916, the Hromada Club was formed, which became the Ukrainian League of Philadelphia in 1925. In 1943, the Ukrainian League of Philadelphia rented out space for the celebration of the liturgy. Before World War II, a Ukrainian school was started.

The newly arrived immigrants organized St. Mary Protectress Ukrainian Orthodox Church (Pokrova) in 1950. At first, it was located on Masher Street, but by 1965, the community moved to Twelfth Street and Sixty-ninth Avenue. The church sponsors a Ukrainian Saturday school, a choir, a dance ensemble, and a literary club. There were other Ukrainian Orthodox churches in the Philadelphia area, however, each is either independent or belongs to other jurisdictions. Ioan Teodorovych, the Metropolitan of the Ukrainian Orthodox Church, resided in Philadelphia for about five decades.

A Sichovij Striltsi flag is presented to Plast in 1950. This was a flag used using the 1914–1918 struggle for Ukrainian independence. Seen here are, from left to right, Ihor Bohachewsky, Julian Kryszanowsky, Ihor Shust, Yaro Hladkyj, Vsevolod Isajiw (kneeling), Nicholas Krawciw (in back, presently a United States Army general), and Nestor Shust. Plast (a Ukrainian Scouting organization) strives to build patriotic, God-fearing, well-rounded, and self-reliant individuals, principally through self-initiative.

Ukrainian Saturday school was administered by the Ukrainian Teachers Association. The students learned language, literature, and history, as well as culture. The student choir performed traditional songs on many occasions. At the extreme right is Yurij Maczuk, president of the educational council in 1952, introducing the student choir.

A demonstration is announced in 1953. American Ukrainians commemorated the memory of those who died in the 1932–1933 Ukrainian famine/genocide.

Brethren and Sisters Ukrainians

Twenty years ago the Ukrainian Nation made the greatest sacrifice on the altar of martyrdom of Ukraine. The Russian occupant, planning complete collectivization of rural farming in Ukraine, decided to crush the national basis of the incorruptible Ukrainian people and forced upon it a fraudulent famine to carry out its despicable scheme.

In 1932–1933 the vicious Kremlin seized all grain in Ukraine and compelled the stubborn believers in private enterprise to die of starvation thrust upon them.

In that horrible catastrophe, unknown for its brutality in human history, died, nearly 7,000,000 Ukrainians, men, women and children in 8 months.

On the mountains of millions of corpses red Moscow tried to fortify its criminal domination in Ukraine.

The Ukrainians who escaped from bolshevik terror and are now scattered all over the free world, are paying homage to the memory of their brothers and sisters murdered by the worst enemies of humankind.

The Ukrainians in the United States, in particular, are now honoring the memory of victims of that sorrowful event — by mass-meetings and demonstrations.

The Ukrainian organizations and societies of Philadelphia and vicinity, viz. Bristol, Chester, Wilmington, Camden, Millville, Trenton etc., will do honor to the memory of the martyrs—ON MAY 23, by a march through the main streets of Philadelphia and then a mass-meeting at Met Hall.

PLACE OF ASSEMBLAGE: Area, Ukrainian-American Club, 2301 Brown St., Phila. 30, Pa.

TIME OF ASSEMBLAGE: 3 p.m., daylight saving time.

FORMATION: Column of fours.

DIRECTION OF MARCH: East on Brown Street, to 22nd St.; South on 22nd to Benjamin Franklin Blvd.; Southeast on Benjamin Franklin Blvd., and around City Hall, thence North on Broad Street to MET HALL, Broad and Poplar Streets, at which place a mass-meeting will be held to protest the atrocities committed by the Communistic Regime against the Ukrainian people.

All Ukrainians are obligated to take part in this demonstration.

By participating in it you will attest to your sympathy with Ukraine in her distress.

UKRAINIAN CIVIC COMMITTEE

STATEMENT

ISSUED AT THE MANIFESTATION OF AMERICANS OF UKRAINIAN DESCENT COMMEMORATING THE MEMORY OF THOSE WHO DIED IN THE FAMINE OF 1932-33 IN UKRAINE.

(Philadelphia, May 23, 1953)

In 1932 and 1933 a great famine raged in Ukraine taking a toll of nearly 7,000,000 lives. This was not a famine which came about through natural causes, but one artificially created by the Kremlin. The Ukrainian peasants and townspeople resisted the Bolshevik collectivization of their farms and property at that time, and the Communists to wipe out this resistance of the freedom-loving and independent Ukrainians used the inhuman measures of starvation.

The American and European press carried frequent reports on entire populations of Ukrainian villages being deported to Siberia to die horrible deaths of starvation and exhaustion in the slave-labor camps. Those who remained were deprived of all means of sustenance. Thousands of tons of grain were removed from within the borders of Ukraine and the inhabitants of the richest farming land in Europe died of hunger. All offers on the part of the International Red Cross to aid the dying people were met with the vehement denials of the Soviet Russian Government of any need for such aid.

Today, twenty years later, the world has become tragically aware of the real nature of Russian Communism. The lessons of Korea, of Vynnytsia and the Katyn Forest Massacre, of the mass deportation of Greek children, of the brutality of Communist prison camps, of the thousands fleeing into Western Europe from the terror behind the Iron Curtain, all have conclusively shown that the Soviet despots are a menace to mankind, to human rights and dignity.

We, Americans of Ukrainian descent, commemorating upon this occasion the memory of nearly 7,000,000 Ukrainians ruthlessly murdered by the Kremlin in 1932 and 1933 appeal to all our fellow Americans to remain constantly vigilant and aware of the most terrible threat humanity has ever known, to guard against succumbing to false Russian "peace" overtures delivered with the aim of weakening the defenses of the free world, and hereby resolve:

1. to appeal to the freedom-loving people of America to support the Ukrainians and other captive peoples behind the Iron Curtain in their resistance to the Communist regime, and in their struggle to throw off the alien barbaric rule of Communist Russia.

2. to appeal to the United States Congress to establish a special commission to investigate the genocidal practices of the Kremlin perpetrated upon Ukrainians and other nationalities throughout their long and horrible enslavement in the Soviet Union.

3. to appeal to the United States Government for an immediate ratification of the Genocide Convention of the United Nations.

WALTER GALLAN
Chairman of the Manifestation

The government of the United States always supported the Ukrainian claim to genocide by the Soviet regime. Annual proclamations were common in the states that had a Ukrainian population. In Pennsylvania both the governor and the mayor of Philadelphia issued proclamations, and the Senate passed resolutions introduced by both parties. Pres. Ronald Reagan, in a letter to the Ukrainian Congress Committee of America, Philadelphia Branch, dated May 20, 1983, wrote, "You have accepted a sacred task to ensure that our thoughts regarding this great tragedy do not fade and that its lessons are not forgotten."

On Good Friday and Holy Saturday the shroud (*plashchanytsia*) representing the wrapped body of Christ has an honor guard. Until the later 1940s, war veterans performed this duty. After the mass arrival of the new immigrants, youth organizations took over this responsibility. Plast took over this religious commemoration in 1951. Plast in the United States exists wherever any substantial numbers of postwar Ukrainian immigrants have settled, mainly in the large cities. Philadelphia began its activity in 1951.

Sviato Vesny, the annual Plast celebration of the arrival of spring, in 1951 was held on ground adjacent to St. Mary's Cemetery in Fox Chase. Attendees at this campout included, from left to right, Borys Zacharczuk, Maxim Chernyk, Lubomyr Perih, Myron Tokar, and Alexander Chernyk. Later Plast expanded, forming the Chornomorsky Kurin, and all of the above joined. By the late 1960s, they were able to purchase a home at Tenth and Duncannon Streets, which was used for social and cultural events.

Seen here is a theatrical presentation by the Ukrainian American Youth Association (SUM) Drama Club in 1954, commemorating the struggles of Ukrainian Insurgent Army (UPA), which was devoted to the cause of Ukrainian liberation during World War II against both Nazi Germany and Soviet Russia and continued after the war against Soviet Russia. Pictured here are, from left to right, Rozalia Alfawycka, two unidentified, Mykola Bachara (standing), and the narrator Myron Soltys Sr.

SUM and the Organization for the Defense of Four Freedoms of Ukraine continue the Ukrainian tradition by holding an annual *Sviachene* (Easter breakfast) for their members in 1951. The Philadelphia branch of SUM was organized in 1949. It conducts a wide variety of activities for its members, primarily the 6 to 25 year olds, with the purpose of fostering Ukrainian cultural and ethnic identity.

Providence Branch No. 193 sponsored its own radio program besides publishing numerous books. Seen here are, from left to right, (first row) Mykola Pasika, Myron Utrysko, Maria Lada, Hryhor Luznycky, Mykola Cenko, and Mykola Karaman; (second row) Mychajlo Romamchuk and Dmytro Fuchko.

Hanusey's Music and Gift Shop opened on Girard Avenue in 1952. The items for sale ran the entire gamut from flowers to refrigerators, but they specialized in all things Ukrainian, especially music. This is the oldest Ukrainian store still in existence. On the wall above the counter are autographs of Ukrainian recording artists.

Petro Andrusiw, internationally eminent Ukrainian artist, painted the iconostases and decorated the church walls in St. Josaphat's Ukrainian Catholic Church in Frankford. Later Andrusiw represented the Millennium of Christianity in an official painting for the Ukrainian Metropolitan Archdiocese of Philadelphia. (Courtesy of Andre Studio.)

The Ukrainian Catholic League of Frankford, with pastor Rev. Myroslav Charyna (in the middle), was enthusiastic youths who wanted to reactivate St. Josaphat's Ukrainian Catholic Youth Club in 1952. The club was a perennial winner of the Bishop Bohachevsky Trophy for the National Ukrainian Catholic track-and-field competition during the 1930s; they were champions from 1937 to 1939. The aims were to keep the youth involved in the parish and to cooperate in church affairs, to instill sportsmanship, and to instill a true spirit of fellowship.

The first graduating class of the Ukrainian Catholic Cathedral of the Immaculate Conception School was in 1953. From left to right are (first row) Anna Krycka, Pasha Manojlo, Rev. Joseph Batza, Anhelyna Bukach, and Eugenia Domchevska; (second row) Sr. Vincent (principal), Ihor Lysyj, Boris Lada, and Sr. Theophilia; (third row) Yurij Yurchak, Ruslan Khmara, Ihor Bak-Boychuk, and Alexander Chernyk. The school was administered by the Sisters Servants of Mary Immaculate. They also directed several homes for the aged.

Members of the Junior Sodality of the Ukrainian Catholic Cathedral of Immaculate Conception School with their teachers in 1952 are seen here; the teachers in the first row are, from left to right, Sr. Oksana, Sr. Demetriada, Sr. Rose, Rev. Joseph Fedorek, Sr. Theophilia, and Sr. Petrunela. The junior sodality encouraged and promulgated spiritual renewal.

St. Nicholas Parish School in 1953 began with grades 1 to 4. In the back row are the teachers, from left to right, Doris Dee, Rev. Ivan Lebedowych, Maria Morachevska, Rev. Julian Slonsky, and Olympia Hajduczok.

The graduating class of St. Basil's Catholic School in 1953 for the first time consisted of more new immigrants than old. In the center are, from left to right, Mother Zenobia, OSMB; Rev. Basil Makuch; and Sister Vera, OSMB.

Philadelphia hosted the Eucharistic Congress in 1954. The march began at the cathedral and wound its way to the civic center, approximately 40 city blocks each way. Members of Providence are shown returning from the civic center.

The Plast group in the Fairmount section in 1955 presented a Christmas pageant. Seen here are, from left to right, (first row) Tanya Krawciw, Danusia Kazaniwska, Maria Stadnytska, Alexandra Chornobriva, Roma Skochalas, Eva Terletska, Bozhenna Skalchuk, and Hanna Fuchko; (second row) Lydia Rudakewich, Oksana Romaniuk, Irene Homzak, Maria Hajduczok, Oksana Pavlish, and Irene Fil; (third row) Oksana Wanchycka, Daria Fylypowych, Maria Hanas, Irena Woloschuk, Natalia Kowalchuk, Tanya Dyakiv, Nadia Zelechovska, Anna Hasiuk, and Zdana Krawciw.

When the new immigrants first arrived in Philadelphia, cooperation among them was the norm. Both youth organizations, Plast and SUM, took part in an original play written by Ihor Shankowsky, *In the Land of the Past and Present*, in 1954.

Rev. Alexander Tresznewsky (center), pastor of the only Ukrainian Catholic Church in the Society Hill section of Philadelphia, poses with the 1954 board of trustees.

Rev. Antonin Ulanitsky organized St. Josaphat's Sacred Heart of Jesus Society in 1948 for young married women. The 1953 members are, from left to right, (first row) Alfreda Halasa, Helen Lopatska, Rev. Myrosalv Charyna (spiritual director), Emelia Szanajda, and Anastasia Klakowicz; (second row) Maria Pokropska, Ahaphia Butenis, Maria Mucowska, Paraskevia Wisniawska, Anna Semsey, and Maria Szydlowska. Through prayer and religious devotion the St. Josaphat's Sacred Heart of Jesus Society aimed to spread the glory of God and to gain salvation for their souls.

Antin Rudnytskyj (first row in middle), the choir director of the Ukrainian singing society Kobzar, poses in 1954 with the choir at a performance.

Rev. Basil Holowinsky, pastor of Christ the King Ukrainian Catholic Church, commissioned Petro Andrusiw to make a copy of the miraculous icon of Our Lady of Zarwanytsia. The copy was installed to the left of the main altar and blessed by Patriarch Josyf Slipyj in 1973. Another miraculous icon, a copy of the Crucifixion also by Andrusiw was placed to the right of the main altar. Icons are venerated in all Eastern churches.

Providence Branch No. 218 was organized in Nicetown as a building committed for the new Christ the King Ukrainian Catholic Church. This church was designated as a full pilgrimage church in 1974, with a copy of the miraculous icon of Our Lady of Zarwanytsia. Petro Andrusiw painted a copy of the icon in 1954. Seen here are, seated from left to right, Mykola Krywucky, Michael Dziuban, Lonhin Markiv, Rev. Basil Holowinsky, Iwanna Fedoriv, and Ivan Sharan.

Plast Day is a celebration of spring. Eugenia Domchevska (kneeling) and, from left to right, Martha Bohachewska, Christine Luznycka, and Christine Dubulak are awaiting the arrival of visitors for this festivity. Plast aims to assist its members in developing their moral strength, mental alertness, and physical prowess. In addition, it attempts to transmit the Ukrainian cultural heritage, to perpetuate Ukrainian traditions, and to maintain an awareness of Ukrainian history. Finally, it strives to develop a dedication to the principles of individual freedom and human dignity.

Tryzub Ukrainian volley ball champions in 1954 pose in front of Centennial Memorial Building in Fairmount Park. They are, from left to right, (first row) Mykola Pryszlak, Yaroslav Sawchyn, and Lubomyr Trytsetsky; (second row) Daria Wozniak, Volodymyr Zavadovych, Platon Switenko, Ihor Zajac, and two unidentified players.

The Association of Ukrainian Academic Societies (Zarewo) was organized in 1959 to pursue higher education goals and to continue the spread of Ukrainian culture and heritage in Philadelphia. The photograph is from the primary meeting. Seen here are, from left to right, (first row) Oksana Bak-Boychuk, Orysia Maczuk, Theodore Onuferko, Zirka Woloshanska, and Lubomyr Luba; (second row) Nina Klymowska, Ihor Bak-Boychuk, ? Muchyn, and Oksana Wanchycka.

Temple University was the first campus to have a Ukrainian Students' Club. The goal was to acquaint the university community with Ukrainian heritage and culture. The club held arts and crafts exhibits and book displays. The two students in the 1958 photograph, Maria Bak-Boychuk (left) and Bohdan Chaplinski (right), are modeling traditional Ukrainian folk dress during one such event.

Pictured here is the Zoia Markowycz Music School's annual recital in 1956. Shown are, from left to right, (first row) Martha Cisyk, Olha Mychajliuk, Sonia Shewchuk, Yarolsav Slusarenko, Andrij Hnatiuk, Bohdan Kunciw, and Walia Berezena; (second row) Roman Kunciw, Larissa Zaika, Eliza Kenkulis, Eleanor Karpynych, Orysia Babij, Hanusia Evshevska, and Halyna Chajkowska; (seated at the piano) Yurij Lewycky; (standing with flowers) Zoia Markowycz.

Yurij Oransky (center), director of the Ukrainian Music Institute (UMI) Choir, is seen with the choir in its 1956 recital; the UMI Philadelphia branch was founded by the pianist Roman Savycky. Under the longtime direction of Yurij Oransky, it staged important operatic and music-theatrical events and featured philharmonic orchestra concerts at many thematic and commemorative concerts. Among many noteworthy events was the world premiere of the specially commissioned opera Lys Mykyta based on the epic poem by Ivan Franko, with music by Vasyl Ovcharenko.

Pictured here are the winners of the 1958 reading contest held by Moloda Prosvita. The winners are, from left to right, Areta Hajduczok, Bohdan Mizak, Eugenia Domchevska, Eleanora Kulchytska, and Olha Medlowska.

The Moloda Prosvita Drama Club commemorates the 90th anniversary of Prosvita Society in Ukraine in 1958. Pictured above is an original scene entitled *Ukrainian Books on Foreign Soil, the Spirit of Ukraine Lives On*, directed by Wolodymyr Tatomyr.

The Ukrainian Catholic Organization (Obnova), with senior and junior divisions, sponsored annual conferences discussing topics pertinent to the layman and the church especially in the late 1950s. The Ukrainian student movement in Philadelphia is only one of many aspects of the organized Ukrainian student life in the United States. It consists of different student organizations; university, college, and high school clubs; and common interest groups. As its priority, the student movement holds retention and preservation of its national identity and the defense of Ukraine.

Through the efforts of Yurij Maczuk and Volodymyr Gallan, an undergraduate course in Ukrainian literature was offered for the first time in September 1959 at the University of Pennsylvania. The 1959 class included, from left to right, (first row only) Yaroslava Marusyn, Kalyna Tatarska, Yurij Maczuk, Hryhor Luznycky (visiting professor), Bohdan Hasiuk (president of Studetska Hromada), Christian Kulchycky, and Aurelia Sereda.

A living chess game in period costumes and with horses was a treat during the summer camps. Myron Soltys Sr. was the longtime director. SUM has a folk dance group, a vocal or string group, a drama club, and various sports teams, and conducts courses in ceramics, *pysanky* (Easter egg) drawing, woodcarving, and embroidery. SUM sponsored a Ukrainian Saturday school and participated in various campaigns for the restoration of Ukraine's independence and the release of Ukrainian political prisoners in the USSR.

The post–World War II immigrants followed in the footsteps of previous immigrations by organizing choirs, dance groups, and the like. Youth organizations competed to have the best dance group. After the performance on the 10th anniversary of SUM in 1959, this photograph was taken. Mykola Bojchuk (left) was the choreographer, and Stefan Yurczak (right) was the coordinator of the youth group.

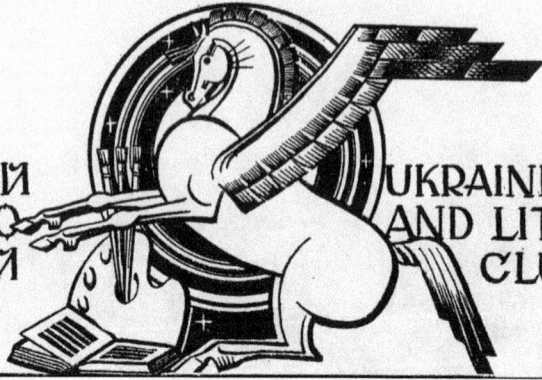

УКРАЇНСЬКИЙ ЛІТЕРАТУРНО-МИСТЕЦЬКИЙ КЛЮБ — UKRAINIAN ART AND LITERARY CLUB

The Ukrainian Art and Literary Club, organized in 1952, discussed and evaluated all aspects of Ukrainian culture, including lectures on various art themes, reviews of literary works, and music recitals. Philadelphia also hosted other more specialized organizations, associations, and societies, including the Ukrainian Library Association of America. Slovo is the association of Ukrainian writers. The association holds annual literary sessions and publishes a collective volume of literary reviews, articles, essays, and short stories.

Annually the Basilian Orchestra, composed of students at Manor Junior College and St. Basil's Academy, honors Metropolitan Andrej Sheptytsky with a concert. As head of the Ukrainian Catholic Church, he sent the Sisters of St. Basil the Great to minister to the immigrants in the United States in 1911.

Areta Hajduczok and Olha Matla perform an Oriental dance during the Irene Holubowska School of Ballet recital in 1954. This school of ballet was formed after World War II. Besides learning classical ballet, the students participated in many theatrical performances. Most of these were held in the Fairmount section at the hall of the Ukrainian League of Philadelphia.

At the annual students ball, a queen of the ball was chosen based on the number of roses she received from admirers during the dance. This custom continued into the mid-1960s. In the photograph, the toastmaster Antin Shutka (by the microphone) is announcing the results. Seen here are, from left to right, Aurelia Sereda, Orysia Maczuk (queen of the 1957 ball) crowning the 1958 queen Christina Charyna, and Martha Shyprykewicz.

Members of the first board of directors of the Ukrainian Teachers Association of Philadelphia pose in 1956; they published a newsletter, conducted pedagogical seminars, and formulated textbooks. The association was affiliated with the local branch of the Ukrainian Congress Committee of America, an umbrella organization. They are, from left to right, (first row) Omelian Hrymaliak, Olena Doroshenko, Yruij Maczuk, Natalia Pazuniak, and Lydia Diachenko; (second row) Wolodymyr Lotocky, Petro Mehyk, Wasyl Cheredarchuk, unidentified, and Wolodymyr Mackiw.

Plast commemorated Ukrainian Independence Day in 1958 by laying a wreath at Independence Hall by the Liberty Bell. Shown here are, from left to right, (first row) Maria Hajduczok, Hania Fuchko, Oksana Pawlysh, Nina Turenko, Melanie Krawchuk, and Chrystia Staruch; (second row) Oksana Romanenchuk, Zdana Krawciw, Irene Kondra, Ulana Lewicky, Daria Fylypowich, Maria Stadnycky, unidentified, Natalia Skochylas, Danusia Kazaniwska, Roma Skochylas, Christine Krochmaliuk, and Ksenia Fedoriw.

Principal Ukrainian newspapers and periodicals were published in Ukrainian and in English in Philadelphia. Foremost of these was *America*, published since 1914, and the *Way*, which began in 1939. Both newspapers are still published in both languages. Other newspapers with shorter life spans dealt with particular facets of life in Philadelphia, emphasizing sports, business, theater, and so on. They also informed readers of news and activities in Ukraine.

Administrative and editorial staffs of *America* along with the printing press staff of Providence are pictured here in 1961. The staff members are, from left to right, (first row, sitting) Ivan Trytiak, Mykola Pasika, Mstyslav Dolnycky, Evhen Zyblikevics, Hryhor Luznycky, Ihnat Bilynsky, and Wolodomyr Wisner; (second row, standing) Omelian Jaremko, Mychajlo Ferkuniak, Stephan Mykytka, Anna Demjanik, Roman Shwed, Wasyl Doroshenko, and Teofil Rudakewicz.

Petro Hursky directed the initial concert of the Association of American Youth of Ukrainian Descent (ODUM) Bandura Ensemble at the Ukrainian Orthodox Church Hall on Mascher Street in 1967. Hursky, first row, seventh from left, established and teaches at the Bandura School. The bandura is the national instrument of Ukraine.

The Ukrainian American Sports Organization women's volleyball team for 1961 is shown here. The team members are, from left to right, (first row) Daria Zawadowich, Roksolana Sira, and Ada Kudenko; (second row) Olena Bajlow, Evhenia Nowakiwska, Luba Silecka, and Nadia Kudenko.

The Ukrainian Democratic Party is seen at the June 1960 national convention held at the Benjamin Franklin Hotel. Most of the Ukrainian Americans who arrived in Philadelphia belonged to the Democratic Party, partly because Philadelphia is a Democratic Party city and partly because they identified themselves with democracy. The Ukrainian Republican Party consisted of a minority of second- and third-generation entrepreneurs and professionals.

The Ukrainian club on Lawrence Street was organized in 1914 by Peter Shetelynetz; becoming financially self-sufficient in the 1920s, the club helped families and sent donations to the needy in the old country. It purchased five bells for the church in the village of Klymetz. After World War II, it offered affidavits to the DPs to help them immigrate to the United States. Members who were especially active were Wasyl and Frank Mychynka, Ivan Demianyk, and Stefan Salapata. The photograph is from 1962.

ODUM's annual celebration of the Ukrainian Sea, *Chornomorske Sviato,* involved a special performance on the make-believe ship *Ukraina* in 1954. The Black Sea has a vital place in Ukrainian history and folklore.

Ukrainian Music Institute of America faculty are shown during the 1960 to 1962 season. The seated first row consists of, from left to right, Roxolana Ogrodnik, Nadia Nedilska, Yurij Oransky, Anastaziya Ogrodnik, Roman Sawycky, Mykola Fomenko, Inna Chernyachiwska, and Bohdan Perfecky.

74

Members of the Ukrainian schools and youth clubs gather at a masquerade party in 1960. This was the main attraction of the new immigrants of the 1950s because they resembled the traditional Ukrainian religious and civic customs.

The Ukrainian National Women's League of America (Soyuz Ukrainok) Branch No. 43 executive board in 1962 included, from left to right, (first row, seated) Anna Bohachewska, Nina Karpynych, Anastazia Zylawa, Osypa Hrabowenska, Leonia Fedak, and Iwanna Subtelna; (second row, standing) Olha Kowalchuk, Stefania Sonewytska, Alexandra Yackewych, Iwanna Osidach, Maria Yewsewska, Stefania Bernadyn, Nadia Oranska, Ania Maksymovich, and Anna Suchy.

The immigrants who came to the United States after World War II started to form their own organizations. At first, their aim was to gain freedom for Ukraine. Eventually these became social clubs when the younger generation took over. Branch No. 77 of Providence was formed in 1962. The original members are, standing from left to right, Bohdan Kulchyckyj, Renata Sharan, Wasyl Zin, Christine Kulchycka, Wolodymyr Wanchycky, Ewhenia Metanchuk, Ihor Chuma, Zdana Krawciw, and Ilarion Chaban.

When Ukrainians started to arrive after World War II, Ukrainian Hall was always filled to capacity for every event. Interestingly, whether they were priests, professionals, the young, or the old, all came to see whatever performance was offered.

In 1960–1961, the Ukrainian Nationals became the United States soccer champions. This was a great event for Ukrainians in the United States since most major media carried it and gave exposure to the event. The 1963 championship team included, from left to right, (first row) Michael Noha, Ricardo Mangini, Ismail Ferreyra, Walter Chyzowych, John Scott, and Edward Tatotian; (second row) Alexander Ely, John Borodiak, Nazar Warwariuk, Eugene Krawets, Oscar Ferreyra, Andrew Rach, Leonard Oliver, Carl Yakovino, Alex Svich, and Vistyslav Glisowic (coach).

The alumni and friends gathered in Philadelphia in 1964 to commemorate the centennial of the University of Chernivtsi in Ukraine. Members of Kozatstvo Chornomore, the alumni association, remember their school days with vestiges of their school uniforms.

The women's auxiliary branch of the Organization for the Defense of Four Freedoms of Ukraine (ODFFU) poses with the board of directors in 1967, with Stefania Sharan (center), the president. Their goal is to promulgate Ukraine's right to freedom of speech, freedom of religious worship, freedom from want, and freedom from fear.

An important religious cultural occasion is the annual *Sviachene*. Seen here in 1964 are, from left to right, Maria Luba, Mary Hanusey Anna Mokerniuk (standing), Rose Woran (unidentified), Joseph Woran, and Joseph Hanusey. Mary and Joseph Hanusey pioneered the *Ukrainian Voice* hour in 1939. Ukrainian radio programs followed, hosted by Theodore Swystun, Wolodymyr, and later Ewdokia, Blavacka, and Myron Utrysko and others. These programs include classical and contemporary music, news from Ukraine, local community events, and literary segments.

Theatrical montage *November 1918* was presented by Theater on Friday, under the direction of Wolodymyr Shasharowsky. In the tableau are, from left to right, Vera Lewycka, Bohdan Pazdrij, Maria Lysiak, Julia Shasharowska, and Yarolsav Pinot-Rudakewych.

The Soyuz Ukrainok Branch No. 10 was organized in 1953 in the Fairmount section; members formed an embroidery school and a literary club. Members of the executive board are, from left to right, (first row) Stefania Chorpita, Irene Petrowska, Natalia Lopatynska, Rostyslava Matla, Olia Cehelska, and Olimpia Hajduczok; (second row) Stefania Makuch, ? Wowk, Ivanna Gentosh, ? Rubel, ? Kostiuk, Maria Shumska, Oksana Rudakewych, and ? Kurchaba.

Branch No. 20 of the Soyuz Ukrainok was founded in 1948. Members of the executive board are, from left to right, Rozalia Kohut, Sviatoslava Barusevich, Wolodymyra Cenko, Mychajlina Chajkowska, Maria Seneyko, Maria Cochran, and Ania Litynska. This very active group exemplified itself in literary roundtable discussions, in staging concerts, in art exhibits, and in political activism. Annually it exhibited traditional Ukrainian costumes from the various regions of Ukraine.

TUSM is the Ukrainian Student Organization of Mykola Mikhnowsky (Mikhnowsky was a political ideologist and philosopher). TUSM publishes the journal *Phoenix*. The photograph is from 1962.

This is the Ukrainian club in the southwestern section of Philadelphia in 1962. Anna Boyko formed this club in 1947. It was very active from the 1950s through the 1970s.

Branch No. 42 of the Soyuz Ukrainok was very active sponsoring lectures and field trips; it also sponsored literary evenings, inviting not only Philadelphia Ukrainian community activists but also individuals of international fame. It also sponsored international humanitarian events.

Officers of the American Ukrainian Citizens' League of Frankford pose in 1969. Seen here are, from left to right, (first row) Damian Zazulak, Osyp Kusen, Omelian Barylko, Mychajlo Maychuk, and Osyp Smoczylo; (second row) Lev Halas, Jakiw Nykyforuk, Walter Oleshycky, ? Lypka, Steven Uryniuk, and Jaroslav Woloszczuk. The club was organized in 1927 to unite people of Ukrainian descent and heritage. They founded a library and organized courses in the English language and for American citizenship.

League of Ukrainian Americans of the Fairmount community board of directors pose in 1967. They are, from left to right, (first row) Myroslav Petriw, Dmytro Matkowsky, Osyp Bakaj, Wasyl Tytanych, Mychajlo Kurylak, Teofil Kulchycky, and Ivan Skalczuk; (second row) Evhen Bilynsky, Mychajlo Cybak, Bohdan Kazaniwsky, Yakim Potiatynyk, Ivan Woloshczuk, and unidentified.

Ukrainian Philadelphians participate in the Folk Fair at Convention Hall. They tell their heritage as woven into the history, folk tales and legends, and of course, the arts and crafts. Sophia Lada, a young Ukrainian Philadelphian who went on to international recognition, created this advertisement in 1966.

Before World War II, students assembled in their respective clubs and at the International Institute known to Ukrainians as the Ukrainian Cultural Center. After World War II, students formed Ukrainian clubs at their colleges and universities. Clubs were formed at Manor Junior College, Drexel University, the University of Pennsylvania, Temple University, LaSalle University, and Villanova University. Seen here is the Ukrainian club at Manor Junior College. Kwitka Semanyshyn (second row, second from left) was president of the organization. Of all the college and university clubs throughout the city, only this Ukrainian club was active on and off campus.

The Ukrainian Gold Cross Christmas pageant was repeated annually in many Ukrainian institutions. Seen here are, from left to right, Sophia Shutka, Maria Kasian, Odarka Turcheniuk, unidentified, Marko Klos, and Yaroslav Shutka.

Nashe Zhytta, a magazine for women published by Soyuz Ukrainok, started in Philadelphia in 1944. The editorial staff in 1959 is, from left to right, Natalia Pazuniak, Lydia Burachynska, Olena Lotocka, Maria Yurkewich, Kekilia Gardecka, and Martha Tarnawska.

Five

UKRAINIAN HERITAGE
AT WORK

With the ongoing development of professional specialization and the establishment of various channels of communications, the Ukrainians of the Greater Philadelphia area today constitute a closely-knit self-containing community, solidly set in an American matrix.
—Peter Stercho, President, Ukrainian Congress Committee of America, Philadelphia Chapter

During the late 1960s, the city of Philadelphia changed and the life of the Ukrainians there did as well. With suburbs constantly growing, the "new" Ukrainian immigrants went along with the flow and started to leave Philadelphia proper. Contrary to their fondest hopes, however, Ukraine had not become free. Their faith in a free Ukraine started to diminish, and assimilation crept in. They began to speak more English than Ukrainian at home; their children Americanized by pure necessity. To the American eye, they joined the great melting pot. They realized, slowly, that the United States would be their permanent home, and certainly that of their children and grandchildren.

Having been professionals in Ukraine, they had far more opportunities for continued education than the immigrants they found here, giving them an edge in acquiring white-collar, professional jobs in America. This gave them an edge in American society and a feeling of importance. As a result, college activities flourished and the sports scene again became important. Ukrainian libraries and reading rooms became active. Literary life excelled in these successful times, and the yearning for homeland was starting to lose its spark. The difference between the generations became more pronounced. The more emphasis the older-generation nationalistic immigrants put on their young during the decade of the 1960s, the more they met with resistance from the youth during the decades from 1970 to 1990. Even the Eastern Rite churches noticed these changes. The larger Ukrainian institutions continued to exist, but barely successfully, while the smaller ones struggled to survive. To combat this troublesome situation, the seven smaller Ukrainian Saturday schools were combined. Many institutions and clubs chose to centralize activities at the UECC, using it as their headquarters. The American way of life started to have the upper hand. Only the Ukrainian Democratic and Republican clubs saw an increase in membership. It was time for the Ukrainian Americans in the Greater Philadelphia area to do some soul searching.

The Kobzar mixed choir, with Antin Rudnytsky (eighth from left) and accompanist Roxolana Harasymowych (ninth from left), is seen here in the 1970s.

Plast vocal group Nezabutky, popular during the late 1960s and into the 1970s, performed for Ukrainian and American audiences. From left to right are (first row) Lydia Lukianovich, Halyna Mazurok, and Daria Korzeniowska; (second row) Rostyslava Odezynska, Motria Czornobil, Christina Romaniw, Nika Fedak, Roksolana Novosad, Ulana Kulyniak, Myroslava Odezynska, and Maria Borysiuk.

The Solovejki Trio, under the artistic direction of Prof. Zoya Markowycz and the vocal direction of Olena Shyshacka, toured Ukrainian communities throughout the United States and Canada. The Solovejki Trio, an SUM group, performed at Philadelphia's summer concert series at Robin Hood Dell in 1972. Seen here are, from left to right, Lesia Leskiw, Marianne Humeniuk, and Myroslava Nowakiwska.

The executive committee of ODFFU, Branch No. 6, is seen here in 1977. It organized protests and demonstrations against Soviet domination of Ukraine. Pictured here are, from left to right, (first row) Myron Utrysko, unidentified, Stefan Wolaniuk, Mychajlo Kowalscyn, Wolodomyr Powzaniuk, Mychajlo Majchuk, Dmytro Rushchak, Andrij Kushnir, and Peter Tkach; (second row) Bohdan Kazaniwsky, unidentified, Myron Ilnytsky, unidentified, Ivan Krych, Wolodomyr Tkach, Mykola Besaha, Yaroslav Bernadyn, Ivan Skalchuk, Myron Hanushewskyj, Bohdan Siletsky, and Peter Mirchuk.

The dedication of the Taras Shevchenko Park at Old York Road and Broad Street in the Nicetown section took place on March 15, 1970. Taras Shevchenko is the national poet of Ukraine.

The Nativity of Our Lord Jesus Nursery on Franklin Street is under the direction of the Missionary Sisters of the Mother of God who have labored in the field of education, especially music and art. A Christmas party at the nursery school in 1973 is seen here; Sister Nadia is at left, and Sister Evhenia is at right. The nursery school provides a much-needed resource for working parents with children under school age.

The Ukrainian Art Studio was founded in 1952 with the purpose of giving students the fundamentals in Ukrainian artistic culture as well as world arts, including their historic development. The school expanded to include more instructors and even to purchase its own building in the Fairmount section. Here are, from left to right, Stefan Rozok, Petro Kapshuchenko, Leonid Molodozhanyn and his wife, Vasyl Doroshenko, Petro Mehyk, and Petro Andrusiw. Mehyk published the *Ukrainian Art Digest* for 27 years.

Seen here is a session of the Philadelphia branch of the Shevchenko Scientific Society. Pictured are, from left to right, (first row) Natalia Pazuniak, Rev. Zenon Zlochowskyj, Bohdan Romanenchuk, Rosalia Szul, and Hryhor Luznycky; (second row) Roman Maksymowych, Alexander Chernyk, Wolodymyr Pushkar, Yaroslav Zalipsky, Michael Dymicky, and Andrij Szul.

Begun in 1952 with just 223 members, the Ukrainian Selfreliance Federal Credit Union has increased to over 5,000 members and five offices. It has received awards for excellence from the National Credit Union Administration. The building on Cottman Avenue is the home office. The Ukrainian Selfreliance Federal Credit Union donates to all Ukrainian humanitarian purposes.

The School of Language and Religion at Pokrova Ukrainian Orthodox Church was started on Berk Street and Germantown Avenue and then moved to Masher Street. Annually a literary competition is held. The 1968 participants display their awards. The pastor Rev. Mychajlo Borysenko is in the center.

Though the cathedral had not been finished, the visit of Patriarch Josyf Slipyj was a festive and solemn occasion in 1973. Standing before the altar are, from left to right, Rev. Walter Paska (later named bishop), Bishop Basil Losten, Bishop Joseph Schmondiuk, Patriarch Metropolitan Josyf, Ambrose Senyshyn, Bishop Isidore Borecky, Bishop Innocent Lotocky, Rev. Myroslav Charyna, Rev. Basil Holowinsky, Rev. Myron Kozmowsky, Rev. Robert Moskal (later named bishop), and Rev. Martin Canavan.

Here the Soyuz Ukrainok Choir, from the Fairmount section, poses in 1973 with choir director Irene Chuma.

Joseph Schmondiuk, born in western Pennsylvania, was an orphan reared at St. Basil's Orphanage. He was ordained to the priesthood by Bishop Constantine Bohachevsky, and in 1956, he was consecrated auxiliary bishop of Philadelphia. In 1961, he was chosen eparch of Stamford, and in 1977, he was appointed metropolitan archbishop of Philadelphia. He died on December 25, 1978. He was the first American-born metropolitan of the Ukrainian Catholic Church in the United States.

Sisters of St. Basil the Great administer Manor Junior College (left), now a coeducational institution, and the library (right) in Fox Chase/Jenkintown. The library houses the Ukrainian Heritage Studies Center.

Since 1954, a favorite event sponsored by the Ukrainian Engineers Society has been the annual debutant ball. The 1972 debutants are, from left to right, Anita Fedak, Christina Romaniw, Larissa Korsun, Maria Odezynska, Nina Wolchasta, Renia Cehelska, Motria Czornobil, Lydia Lukianovich, Christine Kozak, Daria Korzeniwska, Daria Stebelska, Nadia Cehelska, and Rostyslava Odezynska. Besides conducting the annual debutant ball, the Ukrainian Engineers Society generously supported the local civic Ukrainian institutions, especially in the fields of education and publications.

The Lypynsky East European Research Institute was founded in 1963 by Ewhen Zyblikewych and named after Viacheslav Lypynsky, Ukrainian philosopher and political thinker. More than 50 archives of prominent Ukrainians, from here and abroad, are found at the institute. The most significant materials are the archives of Hetman Pavlo Skoropadsky. The institute publishes historical documents, and the library is available for research.

The Élan Vital Conference Committee of the 28th UNA Conference in Philadelphia poses in 1974. Committee members are, from left to right, (first row) John Odezynsky (Republican politician and president of the Ukrainian Republican Party), Stefan Hawrysz (eminent member of UUARC), Walter Galan, Bohdan Hnatiuk, and Iwan Skalchuk; (second row) Mychajlo Kowalchuk, Alexander Yaremko, Iwan Skoczylas, and Michael Nytsch.

This photograph was taken at the 1978 seminar "Ukrainian Physicians in the United States." St. Sophia's Religious Association of Ukrainian Catholics hosted the seminar at its headquarters in Melrose Park. Rev. Taras Lonchyna, the spiritual director, is fifth from the left in the front row. Participants of the seminar were mostly members of the Philadelphia branch of the Ukrainian Medical Association of North America.

Ukrainian Catholics protest the treatment of Patriarch Josyf Slipyj by the Vatican in 1978. The Patriarchate Ukrainian Catholic Church is a militant lay organization, founded in 1965 for the promotion of the patriarchal system in the Ukrainian Catholic Church, with Josyf Slipyj being the first patriarch. Patriarch Josyf visited Philadelphia in 1973 and again in 1976. He is considered spiritual leader of the Ukrainians in diaspora and gave hope to the catacomb church in Ukraine.

During the 1960s and 1970s, there were many protests against Soviet incarcerations of Ukrainian intellectuals. This demonstration publicized the plight of Valentyn Moroz, who endured a five-month hunger strike while in a Soviet prison. (Committee for the Defense of Moroz.)

Ascension Manor, home for the elderly of the Ukrainian Catholic Archieparchy, is composed of two buildings, Manor I and Manor II. This was the brainchild of Bishop Basil Losten. The senior citizens participate in social and cultural events at UACA Hall, at times traveling to Independence Square to participate in Memorial Day services. The Ukrainian community visits the elderly, honoring them with short presentations, musicals, and annual Christmas caroling.

Rev. Robert Moskal organized two choirs at Ascension Manor in 1979. The choirs sang at special events and during liturgy at the cathedral. Seen here are, from left to right, Walter Hirniak, Barbara Chubatyj, Alina Oleksyn, Msgr. Robert Moskal, Stanislawa Szul, Kathryn Gilmore, and unidentified; (second row) Joseph Bereznicky, Kateryna Sewchuk, Josephine Minchak, Maria Bilozor, Klementine Kulchycky, Maria Lepky, Olga Karwan, Anna Shaghko, Maria Harkawa, and Semen Gerlowsky.

The Press Ball was an annual event for 17 years of all the Ukrainian American press published in the United States. Young, talented ladies vied for the title queen of the ball, representing approximately 20 newspapers. The goal was to raise awareness of Ukrainian publications in the United States and to point out to future generations that there is no freedom of the press or of the Ukrainian language in Ukraine. The queen of the ball and the two princesses were chosen by judges composed of prominent Ukrainian writers, poets, musicians, and artists. The contestants were chosen on the basis of their knowledge of Ukrainian language, history, and culture, and their participation in Ukrainian youth organizations. Every ball had a representative that did not participate in the contest, representing Ukrainian underground press. She was attired in Ukrainian garb with visible shackles symbolizing the forbidden Ukrainian press and language. The 1975 committee was composed of members of the World Federation of Ukrainian Women's Organizations Finance Committee of America and the Association of Ukrainian Journalists who organized and sponsored the event. Seen here are, from left to right, (first row) Ludmyla Chajkiwska, Ewdokia Blawatska, Maria Halij, Ludmyla Wolanska, Wolodymyra Cenko, ? Lasowsky, Maria Charyna, Iwan Kedryn Rudnytsky, Natalia Perfecka, Teofila Hanushewska, Oksana Rudakewych, Zoia Hraur, and Maria Leskiw; (second row) Wolodymyr Melnyk, Kwitka Semanyshyn, Stefania Holinata, Irena Melnyk, Christine Kulchycka, Bohdan Siletsky, Christina Senyk, Nestor Olesnytsky, Olha Mosiondz, Maria Jewsewska, Yaroslawa Baranetska, Iwanna Fedoriw, and Petro Kapshuchenko.

The annual proclamation by the city council of the 1918 Independence of Ukraine is presented to members of the Ukrainian community by Mayor Rizzo in 1974. Pictured are, from left to right, Lida Amaro, Mykola Konrad, Peter Stercho, Rev. Robert Moskal, Mayor Frank Rizzo, Taras Konrad, and Lesya Zajac.

The Cheremosh Dance Company is seen in front of the Independence Mall fountain after bicentennial celebrations. The company publishes *Hutsulshchna*, a periodical.

ukrainian festival

"ECHOES OF UKRAINE"

Echoes of Ukraine, part of the Ukrainian Festival series, was a gift from the Ukrainian Community to celebrate the bicentennial of the United States by presenting Ukrainian culture as part of the cultures that make the mosaic that is the United States.

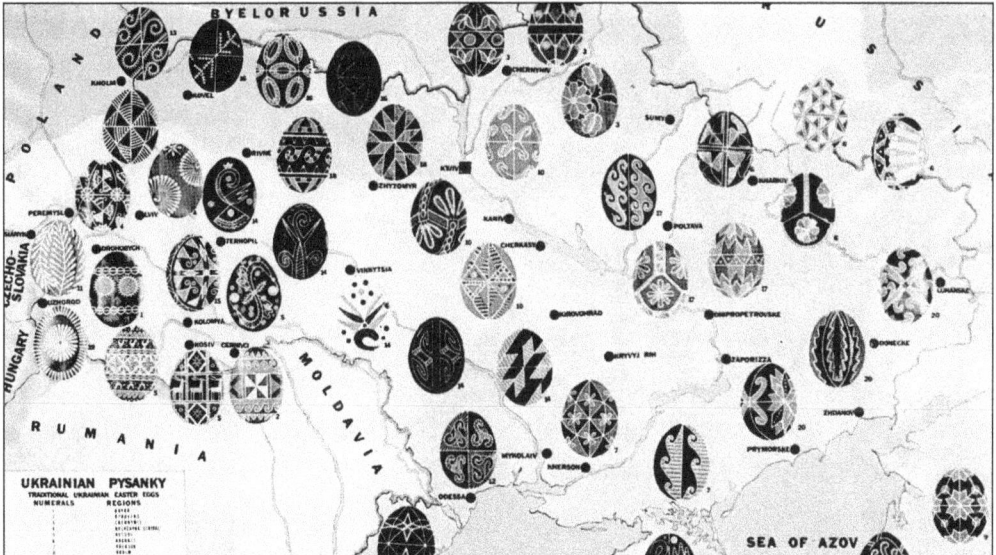

Another way Ukrainians celebrated the bicentennial of the United States was by publishing postcards showing *pysanky* and ethnic dress of the various regions of Ukraine. Symbolic art at its finest is displayed by the *pysanka*, the beautifully decorated Ukrainian Easter egg. With the coming of Christianity in 988, it became part of Ukrainian Easter tradition. The postcards were compiled and drawn by Dzinka Barabach and Sofia Bilynska in 1976.

The St. Sophia's Religious Association of Ukrainian Catholics is a corporation founded by Patriarch Josyf Cardinal Slipyj in 1974. The principal aims of the St. Sophia's Religious Association of Ukrainian Catholics are to ensure growth and development of the Ukrainian Catholic Church and specifically the institutions, which were established or reestablished by Patriarch Slipyj. These include the Cathedral of St. Sophia, the St. Clement Ukrainian Catholic University, and the Church of the Blessed Virgin of Zhyrovytsi and SS. Sergius and Bacchus, all located in Rome.

The Ukrainian Congress Committee of America (UCCA), Philadelphia Branch, was organized in 1946. Longtime presidents were Bohdan Hnatiuk and Peter Stercho. The goal was to bring the plight of Ukraine to notice and seek its liberation. With freedom, the goal changed, and the need for humanitarian aid became foremost. The UCCA, an umbrella organization gathering practically all Ukrainian American institutions and organizations, coordinates the cultural and social activities in each city. This is the Philadelphia board of directors at the 1986 convention.

Zoia Hraur Korsun is cofounder and artistic director as well as choreographer, dancer, and teacher of Voloshky Ukrainian Dance Ensemble. The repertoire of the group ranges from vibrant dances to the graceful and stylized movements. The style is clearly native Ukrainian with classic overtures and technical and acrobatic displays. The costumes are based on original attire. Authenticity for every dance costume is unique, but when appearing in concert Poltava and Hutsul regional dress prevail.

Representatives of Ukrainian newspapers selected candidates to represent them at the Ukrainian Press Ball in 1976. Seen here are, from left to right, Danusia Shebenchak (second runner-up), Christine Shust (queen of the ball), and Larissa Krupa (first runner-up). Shust represented *America*, Philadelphia's Ukrainian Catholic newspaper, at the time a triweekly, which is published by Providence.

The anniversary of the Chernobyl incident, a tragic episode in Ukrainian history, is remembered annually with a prayer service and the lighting of candles in front of Independence Hall. Rev. John Bilanych conducted a prayer service at the 10th anniversary remembrance. This unfortunate global catastrophe, besides taking thousands of lives, made Ukraine a household name to millions of people around the world.

The American Friends of Anti-Bolshevik Block of Nations (AF of ABN) is a coordinating center for anticommunist émigré political organizations from Soviet and other socialist countries with the goal to dismember the Soviet Union into national states. Members of the AF of ABN visited congressman Robert Borski (seated) in 1987. Seen here are, from left to right, (standing) Yury Nakonechny, Vera Nakonechna, and Leo Halas; (standing in back) Yurij Holiney, Lew Iwaskiw, William Nezowy, Ihor Smolij, and Bohdan Todoriv.

Pope John Paul II delivered a homily in the Cathedral of the Immaculate Conception during his visitation in 1979. After the liturgy, Pope John Paul II greeted the multitude of Ukrainian Americans welcoming him outside the cathedral.

At festivities commemorating the Millennium of Christianity in Ukraine in 1988 are, from left to right, Stephen Sulyk, archbishop metropolitan, and patriarch Myroslav Cardinal Lubachivsky of the Ukrainian Catholic Church; and Mstyslav Skrypnyk, metropolitan patriarch of the Ukrainian Orthodox Church.

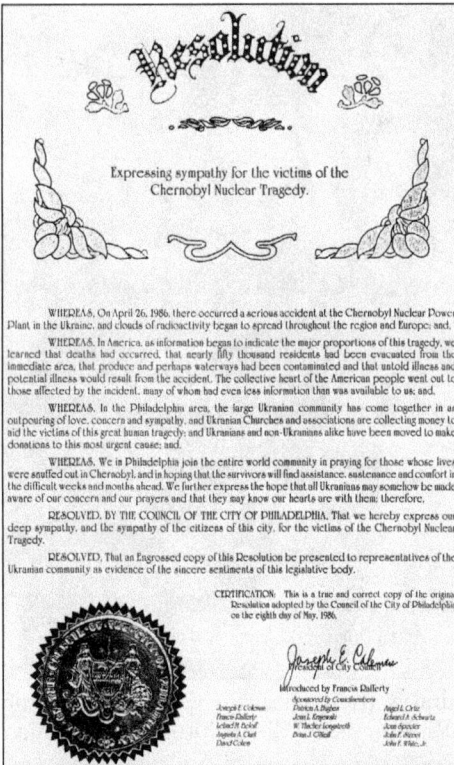

Resolution

Expressing sympathy for the victims of the
Chernobyl Nuclear Tragedy.

WHEREAS, On April 26, 1986, there occurred a serious accident at the Chernobyl Nuclear Power Plant in the Ukraine, and clouds of radioactivity began to spread throughout the region and Europe; and.

WHEREAS, In America, as information began to indicate the major proportions of this tragedy, we learned that deaths had occurred, that nearly fifty thousand residents had been evacuated from the immediate area, that produce and perhaps waterways had been contaminated and that untold illness and potential illness would result from the accident. The collective heart of the American people went out to those affected by the incident, many of whom had even less information than was available to us; and.

WHEREAS, In the Philadelphia area, the large Ukranian community has come together in an outpouring of love, concern and sympathy, and Ukranian Churches and associations are collecting money to aid the victims of this great human tragedy; and Ukranians and non-Ukranians alike have been moved to make donations to this most urgent cause; and.

WHEREAS, We in Philadelphia join the entire world community in praying for those whose lives were snuffed out in Chernobyl, and in hoping that the survivors will find assistance, sustenance and comfort in the difficult weeks and months ahead. We further express the hope that all Ukranians may somehow be made aware of our concern and our prayers and that they may know our hearts are with them; therefore,

RESOLVED, BY THE COUNCIL OF THE CITY OF PHILADELPHIA, That we hereby express our deep sympathy, and the sympathy of the citizens of this city, for the victims of the Chernobyl Nuclear Tragedy.

RESOLVED, That an Engrossed copy of this Resolution be presented to representatives of the Ukranian community as evidence of the sincere sentiments of this legislative body.

CERTIFICATION: This is a true and correct copy of the original Resolution adopted by the Council of the City of Philadelphia on the eighth day of May, 1986.

President of City Council

Introduced by Francis Rafferty
Sponsored by Councilmembers

Joseph E. Coleman   Francis A. Rafferty   Angel L. Ortiz
Francis Rafferty   Joan L. Krajewski   Edward J. Schwartz
Leland M. Beloff   W. Thacher Longstreth   Jean Spencer
Augusta A. Clark   Brian J. O'Neill   John F. Street
David Cohen   John F. White, Jr.

The Chernobyl nuclear tragedy of 1986 is commemorated annually by various Ukrainian organizations. The Philadelphia community also observed this devastation with a resolution in city council on May 8, 1986, introduced by councilman Francis Rafferty.

Since the breakup of UNA in 1910, Ukrainian Fraternal Association (then called Ukrainian Workingmen's Association, with headquarters in Scranton) had many branches in Philadelphia. In commemoration of its 70th anniversary in 1980, four distinguished Philadelphians received honorary citations; they are, from left to right, Mykola Boychuk, Volodymyr Wasylasshczuk, Dmytro Motruk, and Mykola Nykish.

When Volodymyr Blavatsky, prominent Ukrainian stage actor and director, came to Philadelphia in 1950, he organized a theater group (called the Ukrainian Theater Guild) composed of professional actors. It staged many classical performances. After his death in 1953, the group was under the direction of Volodymyr Shasharowsky and later was renamed Theater on Friday. The photograph was to commemorate the 30th anniversary of its founding.

St. Sophia's Religious Association of Ukrainian Catholics Board of Directors pose in 1980. They are, from left to right, (first row), Tatiana Cisyk, Myroslav Cardinal Lubachivsky, and Roma Nawrockyj; (second row) Albert Kipa, Irma Kostyk, Leonid Rudnytzky, and Julian Holowchak.

In late 1970, the younger members of Tryzub started to build a sports complex outside Philadelphia with sports fields for future soccer programs. The facility is available year round for public and private gatherings and picnics in the summer. Since 1995, the annual commemoration of Ukrainian independence has been celebrated here.

In 1988, sports enthusiasts agreed to hold the Second Ukrainian Olympiad at Tryzub's sports complex. The first was held in Philadelphia in 1936 and was such a success that every year until World War II similar sporting competitions were held, however, they were never called Olympics until 1988. Among the medal holders for the track-and-field competition are, from left to right, Christine Sawycka, Tatiana Cyhan, Tanya Lysyj, Vera Kaminska, and Martha Kunash.

Ukrainian and American flags were presented to SUM by representatives of Providence at Youth Day in 1988. Seen here are, from left to right, Daria Nakonezna, Myron B. Soltys, Bohdan Todoriv, Yurij Nakoneczy, Myroslav Petriw, Vera Gramiak, and unidentified.

Annually Ukrainian American Veterans present American flags on Memorial Day at various Ukrainian centers. In 1983, a flag-raising ceremony was held at Ascension Manor with representatives of Providence and the senior citizens.

Tamara Feszczak was crowned Pennsylvania Miss Teen on August 2, 1986. From the early 1930s, Ukrainian clubs selected among their members a Ukrainian queen. There were various qualifications to be the winner. At times these women represented the Ukrainian community in local parades. Later on, other Ukrainian centers continued this tradition, even arranging balls to select a queen of the ball. Many Ukrainian beauty queens were selected outside of Philadelphia, especially in the Ukrainian summer resorts.

UUARC was active in settling post–World War II immigrants and in sending assistance to Ukrainians in need who were scattered around the world. With an independent Ukraine, its resources are in constant demand. Wherever Ukrainians are located they can count on UUARC for needed aid. The board of directors of UUARC in 1986 included, from left to right, (first row, seated) Alexander Tatomyr, Peter Stercho, Irene Kachaniwska, Oleksander Bilyk, Bohdan Hnatiuk, and Ivan Skalchuk; (second row, standing) Mykola Kawka, Metodij Borecky, Myron Baranetsky, Mychajlo Kowalchyn, ? Kolinko, and Mykola Cenko.

Six

MAINTAINING

FAMILY TIES

(Ukraine) …just being "free" is not sufficient, History has shown that Freedom is just a start—we must (help in every way we can to) build a sound, respected nation, to equal the prestige and respect which western countries have achieved.
                                                                —Boris Zacharczuk, President UECC

The unexpected happened in the lives of the Philadelphia Ukrainians; the Soviet Union disintegrated. Signs of this long-hoped-for event appeared sporadically in the late 1980s but were often dismissed as pipe dreams. It was only in 1990, a year before independence, that Ukrainian Americans in Philadelphia began to explore their unique role in this much-awaited event. Disenchanted by now, many did not believe this was happening. One fateful day in 1991, however, life changed completely with the independence of Ukraine proclaimed. The older-generation Ukrainians were ecstatic. They were willing to act by either returning home or at least giving Ukraine their cherished mementos, including books, icons, and such, which they had held on to for this imminent occasion. Needless to say, monetary aide increased. Their American-born children, almost immediately, were granted access to the land of their forefathers or began investing in the new country. The young, recognizing the potential of a sovereign Ukraine, immersed themselves in everything Ukrainian.

The independence of Ukraine influenced the Ukrainian Americans in another unfamiliar way. The Iron Curtain, closed for 50 years, had suddenly opened. For the first time in history, Soviet Ukrainians had a chance to emigrate from their land. Hearing stories about American democracy, and the accompanying riches to be found, they began to go there. The primary motivation was to improve their economic situation. Their composition was considerably different from the previous generations who had settled before them. By necessity, they were well-read in Soviet communism but had little real knowledge of pre-Soviet Ukraine or of the United States. Contrary to former immigrants, their interests lay in America first, not in Ukraine. To the neophyte, their *etat d'esprit* is Ukrainian, but not necessarily patriotic. Being raised in the Soviet tradition, their spiritual life is at best "progressive." Their focus is purely economic. Their knowledge of the Ukrainian language and traditional Ukrainian culture exists, although at times it is attenuated by their communist upbringing. This latest wave swelled the number of Ukrainians in Philadelphia by at least 20,000 and in so doing, created yet another branch of Ukrainian life in Philadelphia.

Today Ukrainian American life centers around the UECC. Due to its history, size, and geographical location, it conducts, promotes, and supports a myriad of cultural, educational, civic, and social programs and services for all ages. Presently more than 37 diverse organizations are linked under the UECC umbrella. Together with the surrounding clubs and churches, UECC provides a ritual connection and a source for fraternization for the several waves of Ukrainian settlements in Philadelphia that are more than a century old.

The UECC, in Jenkintown, was purchased in 1980 and has been serving the community since 1981. Today the UECC houses 36 institutions, among them Ukrainian Heritage School, and is the center of Ukrainian social and cultural activity in the Philadelphia area. Institutions that have offices there are the Ukrainian Engineers Society of Philadelphia; Plast Ukrainian Scouting organization; Ukrainian library; Voloshky Ukrainian Dance Ensemble; Ukrainian Women's League of America; Ukrainian youth organization SUM; and Ukrainian American Veterans.

Founders and past presidents of the Ukrainian Engineers Society of Philadelphia celebrate their 45th jubilee in 1994. They are, from left to right, (first row) Gregory Kuzma, Wolodymyr Shyprykewich, Lidia Diachenko, Lew Yackevich, Wolodymyr Wynnycky, and Bohdan Hnatiuk; (second row) Borys Zacharczuk, Lew Kushnir, Osyp Nimylowich, Roman Cyhan (in back), Eugene Zyblikewych, Wolodymyr Kuzyk, Larissa Zaika, Alexander Bilyk, Ivan Danylenko, Myron Bilas, and Metodij Borecky.

St. Michael the Archangel Ukrainian Catholic Church in Jenkintown is dedicated in memory of Patriarch Josyf Slipyj. It is the only Ukrainian Catholic Church in the Philadelphia area to follow the Julian calendar. At first it was under the jurisdiction of Patriarch Slipyj. Since 2004, it belongs to the Archieparchy of Philadelphia. It was designed in the traditional Ukrainian style and completed in 1992.

Plast treated guests at the 1988 Millennium of Christianity in Ukraine celebration to a representation of life and times in Kievan Rus' in traditional dress of 1,000 years ago. The Ukrainian Americans in Philadelphia celebrated this occasion throughout the entire year with a variety of ceremonies.

The Board of Education Council was formed in 1990, when the two major Ukrainian Saturday schools merged. Ukrainian Heritage School formed the largest Ukrainian Saturday school in diaspora. From left to right are (first row) George Szwabiuk, Lubomyra Kalyta, Albert Kipa, and Vera Shapowalenko; (second row) George Kyzyma, Olha Kuzewich, Ivan Yaworsky, Alexandra Leskiw, and Lew Iwaskiw.

Cheremosh Ukrainian Hutsul School of Dance is shown at the Ukrainian Festival at the Garden State Arts Center in 1991. Pictured are, from left to right, (first row) Wasyl Konowal, Christopher Plachta, Adrian Prociuk, and Nicholas Konowal; (second row) Larysa Leskiw, Ulana Luciw, Natalia Prociuk, Chrystyna Leskiw, and Stefania Fedorijczuk; (third row) Kateryna Bendiak, Katrin Plachtam, Roksana Dawyd, Chrystyna Fedorijczuk, Olexa Horbachevsky, Jurij Fedorijczuk, Dmytro Luciw, Petro Horbachevsky, and Andrij Luciw.

Since 1992, Tryzub has sponsored a festive picnic commemorating the declaration of independence of Ukraine every August with music and international fanfare. The festivities commence with a procession with Cossacks on horseback.

The Prometheus Ukraine Male Choir was founded in 1963 in Philadelphia. It has performed around the world to great acclaim. In this 1995 photograph, members are dressed as Ukrainian Cossacks for an upcoming concert. In the center, from left to right, are Irene Zwarych (accompanist), Adrian Brittan (conductor), and Alexandra Rudyj Penkalska (accompanist).

A medical airlift to Ukraine began in 1991, when *Mriya*, the world's largest cargo plane, arrived at Philadelphia International Airport. Alexander Chernyk, president of Ukrainian Federation of America (UFA), is supervising one of the many humanitarian projects undertaken by UFA.

Ukrainian Heritage Studies Center, administered by the Sisters of St. Basil the Great, houses books, ceramics, *pysanky*, and other examples of Ukrainian heritage. In this 1994 photograph are, from left to right, Sister Frances, OSBM (director of the UHSC); Chrystyna Prokopowych (curator); and Anna Maksymowych (librarian and translator).

World Federation of Ukrainian Women's Organizations Financial Committee of America was formed in 1968 to publish *Ukrainian Woman in the World* and to supply humanitarian aid to orphans in Ukraine. The committee in 1992 was composed of, seen here from left to right, (first row) Maria Jewsewska, Ludmyla Chajkowska, Maria Charyna, and Yaroslawa Baranetska; (second row) Chrystia Senyk, Christine Kulchyckyj, Maria Leskiw, Maria Danyliw, Myroslawa Hill, and Halyna Carynnyk.

Longtime members of Tryzub hold citations after being inducted into the hall of fame in 1998 by Ihor Chyzowych, president (third from left). The inductees are, from left to right, Bohdan Siryj, Mychajlo Jurczak, and Yaroslav Kozak.

Shown here is the Ukrainian Human Rights Committee (UHRC) meeting with Mayor William Green, first lady of Philadelphia Patricia Green, and Human Right Ambassador to the United Nations Jerome Shestack, Esq., to discuss the plight of Ukrainian political prisoners in 1982. Seen here are, from left to right, (first row) Ulana Mazurkevich, Christine Fylypowich, Orysia Hewka, and Vera Andryczyk; (second row) Irene Jurczak, Odarka Turczeniuk, Donna Kulba, Chrystia Senyk, Vera Laschyk, Christine Perfecky, Irene Skulsky, and Sr. Gloria Coleman; (third row) Patricia Green and Jerome Shestack, Esq.

In 1986, Leonid Rudnytsky introduced an undergraduate course in Soviet and East European Studies at LaSalle University. This became the forerunner of the Central and East European Graduate Program in 1993. Both programs cater mainly to students from abroad, especially from Ukraine. Seen here are, from left to right, Rudnytsky with Marta Wasiltsiw and Alexandra Matla, two of the students who completed the course.

Cheremosh Ukrainian Hutsul Society and its board of directors pose in 1996. Their aim is to spread knowledge of their culture and heritage by publishing books, performing native dances, and creating arts and crafts. They are, from left to right, (first row) Ulana Prociuk, Eryna Cvikula-Korchynska, Eudokia Sorochaniuk, Oksana Tkachuk, and Roksolana Luciw; (second row) Dmytro Thachuk, Jaroslaw Fedorijczuk, Dmytro Fedorijczuk, Wasyl Panchak, Wasyl Thachuk, Yurij Fedorijczuk, Dmytro Sorochaniuk, and Michael Luciw.

Members of the executive board of the UFA, seen in 1999, are, from left to right, (first row) Vera Andryczyk, Bohdan Korzeniowski, and Zenia Chernyk; (second row) Walter Maruschak, Andrew Horbowy, Eugene Novosad, Steven Romanko, Albert Kipa, Roman Cyhan, Metodij Borecky, and Ivan Danylenko.

The Ukrainian American Senior Citizens Association meets regularly at UECC. According to its mandate to make life better for elderly people and to encourage independence, it sponsors a variety of activities that range from looking after infirm members to enjoying a cultural outing. Here they are visiting SS. Cyril and Methodius Church in Olyphant, Pennsylvania. Rev. Stephen Hrynuck (in center) is the longtime pastor. Ivan Dubil (second from right) is the longtime organizer of these cultural excursions.

Seen here is a Providence outing on the Delaware River to visit the ship *Ukraine*. Pictured are, from left to right, (first row, kneeling) Oleh Antonyuk and Irene Buczkowska; (second row, standing) Stephanie Wochok, Irina Galey, Oksana Jarymowycz, Ihor Smolij, captain of the ship (unidentified), Myron Soltys, Anna Makuch, and Christina Lytwyn.

The Ukrainian Catholic Cathedral Complex houses the Sheptytsky Educational Center, Byzantine Church Supplies store, Treasury of Faith Archieparchial Museum, Cathedral Hall, and in the garden, a statue of Metropolitan Andrej Sheptytsky, the visionary prelate who recognized the needs of the Ukrainian Americans and appointed Bishop Soter Ortynsky for the United States.

Pictured here is a ceremony dedicating the Alexander Chernyk Memorial Gallery at the UECC in 2001. Participants of the dedication ceremony are, from left to right, Taras Lewytsky, Marijka Tatunchak, Albert Kipa, Patricia Sawchak, and Anatol Prasicky. Chernyk was the founder and first president of the UECC.

The United Ukrainian American Relief Committee was organized in 1944 to provide humanitarian aid to the DPs. By 1945, it gained international recognition for its work. Fund-raising campaigns among the Ukrainian Americans was the basis for helping political refugees. In the postwar period, it assisted not only Ukrainian refugees in their new homelands throughout the Western Hemisphere and Europe, but also those institutions created to maintain their Ukrainian culture and language. With the independence of Ukraine, it expanded its humanitarian efforts.

The Organization for the Rebirth of Ukraine is a nationalistic political organization established in 1931 in the United States. Ideologically it is connected with Ukrainian Nationalists and supported the liberation struggle in Ukraine. Among its programs is Ukrainian Gold Cross for Youth. The 12th branch was founded after World War II. Seen here are, from left to right, (first row) Peter Kluk (chairman), Oleksander Prociuk (president), and Natalia Pazuniak; (second row) Ulana Prociuk, Jaroslaw Zmurkewycz, George Stecina, and Lesia Stecina.

Traditional national costumes are displayed annually. In 1997, the UECC sponsored this compilation of costumes representing native dress from the diverse regions as a Ukrainian mosaic at the Philadelphia Museum of Art. Each region has its own colors, embroidery designs, and styles of clothing. In the past, native costumes were worn throughout the country; later only the village people wore them. Now they are worn with pride at public functions.

Children and teachers of Ukrainian Gold Cross Nursery School greet Archbishop Metropolitan Stephen Soroka (sitting in the middle) as he visited them in 2004. Wolodymyra Kavka, president of the Gold Cross Association, is at the far right.

Ulana Mazurkevich (at the microphone) presents to Mayor Edward Rendell (left) the eyewitness accounts of the tragedy of *Holodomord* (famine/genocide in Ukraine) as remembered by the survivors (seen in front of the podium, listed from left to right) Petro Hursky, Wasyl Yevtushenko, and Ivan Kononenko. Stalin and his Soviet regime, to bend the people to his will, created *Holodomord* in 1932–1933.

Starting in the 1980s, the Ukrainian American Senior Citizens Association was the most active of Ukrainian organizations in Philadelphia. On a weekly basis, members attend lectures on diverse topics. They visit infirm members, volunteer at hospitals, and offer health information regarding the newest in medical research. They offer exercise programs and serve hot lunches for the needy. They support many programs by their volunteer work.

The Glockenspiel Ensemble of the First Ukrainian Evangelical-Baptist Church not only plays these rare instruments but sings as well. In the short time since its inception, the group has perfected its art to such a degree that it is invited to perform at civic events. The group was founded in 2003.

The Basilian Spirituality Center in Fox Chase (Replica from Lviv, Ukraine) is a ministry of the Sisters of St. Basil the Great. Opened in 2000, it offers a sacred place of hospitality for prayer, study, and spiritual renewal.

Leonid Krawchuk, the first president of Ukraine, was invited to speak at the United Nations. Ukrainians invited him to Philadelphia and honored him with a banquet at the Bellevue Stratford Hotel. At the banquet, Krawchuk (at the right), addressed the audience; at his side is his translator Dmytro Markiv. LaSalle University took this opportunity to bestow on him an honorary degree during graduation ceremonies at Convention Hall on this date as well.

Ukrainian printing houses flourished in Philadelphia. First was the Ruthenian Printing Press started by the Sisters of St. Basil the Great, followed by America Printing Press. Later Dnipro Printing Press came into existence, and after World War II a great number of small, local printing houses printed announcements, greeting cards, and other memorabilia in both languages. Here is a sample of Ukrainian or Ukrainian topic books published in both languages in Philadelphia printing establishments.

The Baptist community commemorates its high school graduates with a formal event. The 2003 graduates are, from left to right, Bohdan Fedyk, Edward Pianov, Yulia Login, Nina Kowalczuk, Ina Kisilova, Pastor Dmytro Login, Anna Viniwska, Alla Bondarenko, Ella Pianova, Yaroslav Shymylo, and Pavlo ?.

The Orange Revolution, during the contested Ukrainian elections of 2004, was supported worldwide. Philadelphia Ukrainians joined their countrymen in support of Victor Yushchenko and against the prearranged, Moscow-backed candidate.

The 2005 recipient of the Philadelphia Liberty Medal, Ukrainian president Viktor Yushchenko, said that American democracy inspired him to be firm in his resolution to gain democracy for Ukraine during the Orange Revolution. Edward Rendell, governor of Pennsylvania, is seated on the right.

Ulana Mazurkevich (president of the UHRC) offers a toast to Yushchenko, third president of Ukraine, at the Constitution Center after he was awarded the Liberty Medal on September 19, 2005. Behind her and to the left is the newly formed choir Ukraina, composed of members of various Ukrainian choirs from the city.

Before the influx of the postwar immigrants in 1946, the theatrical play *Ukraina*, staged by the Ukrainian American children at St. Basil's Orphanage, appealed for the freedom of Ukraine, the homeland of their forefathers. The final scene depicts the prayer of the orphans for the liberation of Ukraine. Almost to the day, 45 years later, the orphans' prayers were answered.

Philadelphia Electric Company (PECO) building is pictured here on December 5, 1991; PECO highlights interesting events that affect Philadelphians. These displays, in Center City just off the Schuylkill Expressway, commemorate the independence of Ukraine on August 24, 1991, and were seen for an entire week. There are over 92,000 descendents of Ukrainians living in the Greater Philadelphia area. (This image is time phased.) (Courtesy of PECO.)

Visit us at
arcadiapublishing.com

••

www.ingramcontent.com/pod-product-compliance
Lightning Source LLC
Chambersburg PA
CBHW050605110426
42813CB00008B/2460